The Bitter Life of Božena Němcová

Advance Praise for
The Bitter Life of Božena Němcová

"The Bitter Life of Božena Němcová *by Kelcey Parker Ervick is one of the least bitter, most loving books I have read in a long time, and it's beautifully made. Fans of Jenny Boully's* not merely because of the unknown that was stalking toward them *and Maggie Nelson's* The Argonauts—*frankly, anyone interested in fairy tales and in memory and in desire—should read this haunting biographical collage. It's a terrific work of lyric nonfiction, a form underrepresented on the fairy tale shelves.*"
—KATE BERNHEIMER, author of *How a Mother Weaned Her Girl from Fairy Tales*

"*This multi-genre biographical novel delighted and enlightened me—that research, journalism, imagination, postcards, poetry, archival letters, found raw materials, and imaginative synthesis could result in such a beautifully clear book. Frequently, multi-genre experiments remain experiments—that is, failures—but this book is a huge success. Parker Ervick has transported me to Prague and shown the blending of fairy tales, history, and cultures laying the groundwork for Kafka's surrealism (and exported far away, magic realism). With a touch of magic, Parker Ervick plays with the shrouds of mystery surrounding Božena's life and origins: Was Goya her father or grandfather? Metternich? Her love affairs seem to be worthy of Anaïs Nin. Behind so many imaginative men of letters in Bohemia, it turns out there was one astonishingly creative woman, Božena Němcová. I recommend the book: you will learn, imagine, and enjoy!*"
—JOSIP NOVAKOVICH, author of *April Fool's Day*

The BITTER LIFE *of* BOŽENA NĚMCOVÁ

A Biographical Collage

Kelcey Parker Ervick

Rose Metal Press

2016

Rose Metal Press, Inc.
P.O. Box 1956
Brookline, MA 02446
rosemetalpress@gmail.com
www.rosemetalpress.com

Cataloging-in-Publication Data on file with the Library of Congress.

ISBN: 978-1-941628-07-2

Image credits, works consulted, and publication acknowledgments can be found in the back matter of this book, beginning on page 327.

Cover art by Kelcey Parker Ervick
Cover and interior design by Heather Butterfield
See "A Note about the Type" on page 338 for more information about the typefaces used.

This book is manufactured in the United States of America and printed on acid-free paper.

For my daughter, Monte

Table of Contents

I know in Czech only one music of language, that of Božena Němcová.
                    —Franz Kafka, *Letters to Milena*

A new chapter of our response to her has just begun.
                    —Peter Demetz, *Prague in Black and Gold*

Introduction: This Is Not a Biography

The Bitter Life of Božena Němcová is biographical, but it is not a traditional biography. My favorite "biography" is Virginia Woolf's *Orlando*, which is, of course, not a biography but a novel that humorously exposes the inherent limitations of biography—of the representation of any person, any interior life. As I researched and crafted a narrative of Božena Němcová, a nineteenth-century Czech writer with an unconventional life, I embraced those limitations, along with my limited knowledge of the Czech language, as Oulipian-like constraints that led to a collage-based approach. Thus this project is less of a biography than an excavation and hopefully an unveiling.

Most people fall for Prague's architecture; I fell for its literature. I fell for the stories of Milan Kundera, Franz Kafka, Ivan Klíma, Bohumil Hrabal, Josef Škvorecký, Karel Čapek, Jaroslav Seifert, and Jaroslav Hašek. But they were all men; their stories were of wars and paramours. Božena Němcová was not only a woman writer in a canon of men, but a woman writer who preceded them all, who emerged at a time, in the 1840s, when the only other known Czech female author was Magdalena Rettigová, a writer of cookbooks whose ideal woman was devoted above all to her husband. Němcová, who never felt compatible with the man she married, wrote tales of smart and powerful heroines who defied convention and sometimes suffered for it.

Like most important encounters in my life, I discovered Božena Němcová by chance. ("Chance and chance alone has a message for us," says Milan Kundera in *The Unbearable Lightness of Being*.) In 2003, I went to Prague for the first time, on a whim. I was visiting a friend in Berlin, and she suggested a weekend trip. We toured the castle grounds and St. Vitus Cathedral, where we climbed the spiral staircase to the top of the clock tower. The view of Prague's red roofs spread out before me like a field of poppies in the gray of mid-March. I could see Old Town Square and the Charles Bridge, which we'd crossed to get here. The gray Vltava River had flooded the year before, and there was evidence of its destruction on the walls of many of the buildings in Malá Strana at the foot of the castle's hill. As I stood at the top of a five-hundred-year-old stone clock tower, I felt like a girl in a fairy tale.

One could even say that a spell had been cast upon me, perhaps by the Noon Witch. She may have already bewitched me an hour earlier, as my friend and I joined a hundred other tourists to watch the Astronomical Clock—adorned with saints, serpents, scholars, and skeletons—strike noon in Old Town Square. Perhaps, like Němcová's Divá Bára was said to be, I was put under a spell, destined to spend years reading and writing about Prague, reading and writing its stories.

At the castle's gift shop I purchased a beautifully illustrated copy of *Czech Fairy Tales* by Božena Němcová and Karel Erben for my daughter, who was six at the time. Did I notice, as I paid, that Němcová's portrait was on the 500-crown note I handed to the cashier? I did notice eventually. A woman? On national currency? Who was she? This book is the result of years spent trying to answer that question.

I began my search online, where information was contradictory and poorly translated: Was she born in 1820, 1818, or 1817? Were her parents peasants, or was she the illegitimate daughter of royalty? Such contradictions might be expected on the Internet. I went to my university library and consulted the scholars, searching for Němcová's name in indexes of English-language books about Czech literature and culture. I found primarily short entries that praised her fairy tales and lamented her bitter life. Over and over this came up: her short, bitter life. I found these claims surprising in the context of her writing. Like most fairy tales, her Czech and Slovak stories are full of happy endings. Her 1855 novel *Babička* (*The Grandmother*), subtitled "Scenes from Country Life," relishes in communal stories and the cycles of nature, and, though it ends with the grandmother's death, she is proclaimed a "happy woman" in the famous final words.

As I kept researching, I learned that Němcová's marriage was not happy, and that she had a series of extramarital affairs. The couple's political beliefs made them the target of police, especially after the failed nationalist revolts against the Habsburg Empire in 1848, so the family constantly had to relocate. They had four children, one of whom died of tuberculosis when he was fifteen. A decade later, in 1862, despite the success of *Babička*, Němcová spent the end of her own young life begging for money and food, suffering abuse by her husband, and dying of an aggressive cancer.

Well, I thought, what else could one expect of the life of a woman writer one hundred and fifty years ago? Bitter indeed.

But then I found a book that transformed my perspective. In *Women of Prague* by Wilma Iggers, I encountered a Božena I'd not yet read about: the Božena of her own letters. In her letters she is a new, sad wife, an illicit lover, a worried mother. In a letter to her husband she says she could have had any man she wanted. In a letter to a lover she writes that she denies her husband sex, then she admits to feelings of sexual desire. In her letters, I discovered a voice of intelligence, frankness, and longing, but little of the bitterness I had been led to expect.

When I read these letters, I felt kinship, sisterhood, gratitude. And confusion: Why hadn't I heard of Božena Němcová the way I'd heard of the Brothers Grimm? Why was the available information so contradictory and reductive? Why weren't the rest of her letters translated into English?

The answer is primarily historical: During Němcová's life, the Czecho-Slovak regions of Bohemia, Moravia, Silesia, and Slovakia were part of the Habsburg Dynasty, and these regions did not become an independent Czechoslovakia until 1918, more than fifty years after her death. The country's independence was quickly subsumed, once again, by a century of German and Soviet occupiers, and her stories and letters were hidden behind the Iron Curtain for decades.

Nonetheless, Němcová's influence on Czech writers has spanned generations. Franz Kafka read *Babička*—the first Czech novel—as a student in the 1890s, and critics note its direct influence on his *The Castle* (written in 1922 and published posthumously in 1926). Her letters were published for the first time in 1917 at the height of Kafka's career, and he read and admired them. In 1940, during the Nazi occupation of Prague, František Halas and the future Nobel Prize winner Jaroslav Seifert each wrote a collection of poems about Němcová. In 1993 Milan Kundera called her "The Mother of Czech Prose."

It has not even been three decades since the Velvet Revolution of 1989, so perhaps I am too impatient for a process that will surely take time: the rendering into English of Němcová's letters, of the numerous scholarly books and biographies, of her many untranslated works. When I first began researching Němcová in earnest in 2007, the only version of *Babička* I could find in English was a 1960s translation, mimeographed and bound in a metal clip, at the Indiana University library. When I returned to Prague in 2010, I found Frances Gregor's 1892 translation reissued by the Czech publishing house Vitalis for sale at the Kafka Museum. Slowly, slowly, things are changing. Jack Zipes, translator of the Brothers Grimm tales, and a scholar who has been writing about fairy tales since the 1970s, discussed Němcová for the first time in his 2013 *The Irresistible Fairy Tale: The Cultural and Social History of a Genre*. Articles and dissertations are being written about her in English. Rose Metal Press is publishing this book.

Like Němcová, I am a storyteller, and I wanted to tell her story even if I didn't have access to all of the information and my Czech never much improved. The gaps have become part of the story. The information I gathered came in fragments, and those fragments had strong voices: that of the dismissive scholar, the enthusiastic biographer, the awkward English translator, the experts on radio interviews, the voices of Němcová's husband and lovers, and Němcová's own voices as fairy tale writer, novelist, lover, and letter writer. *The Bitter Life of Božena Němcová* is told entirely through these voices and found fragments. The letters and other first-person reminiscences by her contemporaries are in italics throughout the book. The footnotes identify the source for each fragment. Many footnotes also provide the reader with additional context about the source text, relevant historical figures and debates, and scholarly discussions of Němcová's work. Because so many representations of Němcová are visual—statues, paintings, book illustrations, and even her tombstone—the biographical collage also includes my own travel photographs, postcard-size paintings, and mixed-media collages.

If the main text is an unveiling of Božena Němcová, "Postcards to Božena" is an unveiling of me. As I worked on this book (and in 2012 in particular), my personal life underwent many changes that seemed intrinsically linked to my work on this project. In the summer of 2012, having just gotten tenure at my university job, I enrolled in a month-long Czech language course in Prague. I hoped to learn enough Czech to begin translating Němcová's letters on my own, but instead I humiliated myself on a daily basis by saying things like, *I'm a professor, I'm from America, I ate a car for breakfast.* As I studied her language in the city where she lived and wrote for so many years, I felt more connected to Božena than ever. I was almost forty-two, the age she was when she died. Every day on the bus to and from the Czech class, I passed by the apartment where, according to the plaque, Božena Němcová's *The Grandmother* was written. After a lifetime as the privileged eldest grandchild, I had just lost both of my beloved maternal grandparents. I was with my Granny when she died on Mother's Day just two months earlier. And while in Prague, I took a train to my grandfather's family village in Slovakia, where I was welcomed by his first cousins whom he had never met, and I saw the house where his mother was born. And then, most significantly, I returned home and faced the beginning of the end of my seventeen-year marriage. Inspired by Němcová's letters—and by my friend who advised me to write it all down—I began to compose postcards to Božena, which became a meditation on life, letters, love, and happy endings.

A Few Notes on Czech Names

Božena Němcová was born with the name Barbora Panklová, and was also called by the diminutives Barunka or Barushka. Czechs commonly and affectionately use such diminutives. In an article at expat.cz ("Dos and Don'ts: Names"), Ryan Scott gives the example of a woman named Kateřina, who may be called "Katka, Káťa, Káča, Kateřinka, and Kačenka," depending on the context. As my Czech language teacher said, "We Czechs like to make everything cute and little."

In Czech, women's surnames typically end in *–ová*. So the daughter or wife of Jan Pankl would go by the surname Panklová. When Barbora married Josef Němec, she became Barbora Němcová. I assumed that the addition of the suffix *–ová* was a not-so-subtle way of adding "egg" to a name to feminize it. It's not quite so, though perhaps the spirit is the same: the suffix turns a noun into a feminine adjective, which apparently modifies the masculine noun form. (Only in 2004 did a Czech law pass that a woman could forgo the suffix.)

When she began writing in the 1840s, Němcová changed her first name from Barbora to Božena, which sounded more Czech. This was a common practice for Czech nationalists who sought to publicly affirm their patriotism. In "Mystifications and Ritual Practices in the Czech National Awakening," David Cooper provides context for this Czech ritual: "When confronting a new acquaintance, how should one know whether or not [...] the individual belongs to Czech patriotic society? At times, it could be dangerous to ask. Many Czech patriots chose to mark this rite of passage with an external sign, a signpost indicating their belonging to the Czech nation, by changing their names. Most often, however, it involved the taking of a second name, following the fashion of the times for triple names, in which the patriotic name followed or sometimes replaced the baptismal name: Božena (Barbora) Němcová."

According to rules of Czech declension, names also change when they are used as an adjective rather than as a noun. For example, the Museum of Božena Němcová becomes Muzeum Boženy Němcové.

In Czech, the first syllable is emphasized and a *c* in the middle of a word sounds like *ts* (not *k*). The *haček* over the *ž* turns it into more of a *zh*, and the *haček* over the *ě* adds a *y*-sound between the *n* and the *ě*. The accent over the *á* doubles the length of the vowel sound.

Thus, the proper pronunciation of Božena Němcová is: BO-zhena NYEM-tsovah.

THE BITTER LIFE OF
BOŽENA NĚMCOVÁ

1. Shrouded in Mystery

The Little Stars of Gold, Part One

Once upon a time,
there was a little girl,
six years old, Božena
by name. She was an
orphan. She had no-
thing in the world but
the clothes on her back
and a piece of bread
which her poor god-
father had given her,
when he sent her off
to her aunt.

Alone and forsaken,
she set out for the
village where her aunt
lived in a little hut. It
seemed a great di-
stance to this little girl.
She was timid and
afraid as she trudged
along and oh, so lon-
ely. At a turn in the
road, she came upon
a poor beggar man,
who said, "Little girl,
will you give me so-
mething to eat? I am
very hungry." Instantly,

she gave him the whole piece of bread, without thinking of herself at all, saying—

Němcová, Božena. "Little Stars of Gold." *The Disobedient Kids and Other Czecho-Slovak Fairy Tales.* Trans. William H. Tolman and V. Smetanka. B. Koči, 1921.

The August 1922 edition of Chicago's *Czechoslovak Review* cites this book among its "Publications Received" and notes that, "Parents, with growing children, will find this book of immense help and at the same time aid in preserving the traditions of the Czechoslovaks in this country." Nonetheless, the reviewers question the choice of title: "Why the title of 'The Little Stars of Gold' was not chosen instead of the one selected we cannot understand."

"The Disobedient Kids" is a two-page tale in which a mother leaves behind her four "little ones," telling them not to answer the door unless they hear her voice. Three times a fox asks to be let in, and the third time manages to sound like the mother. The kids open the door and are devoured. The kids in the illustration are goats.

The lineation of this passage reflects the original print version in which the text wraps around illustrated images in the book.

When I Look at the Heavy Gray Fog

at those hollow trees, from which the yellowed leaves fall
one by one—when I observe that vague emptiness, that sadness
everywhere, I feel sad and chilly and

I wish I had wings

so that I could fly like a little bird to warmer, freer, more beautiful
landscapes where a warmer, freer air blows. But when anger and sorrow
force me to shed a real tear,

I cry out to those demons

rushing toward me and wanting to dig into my heart with their claws, to
muddy my blood with their poisonous breath—and I reach for the cup
my good fairies hand me for refreshment.—

They drive away the gloom, turn the gray sky blue and line it with gold;
they dress the earth in a green garment and breathe fresh life into the
wilted blooms—and into that beautiful nature

they magically place the picture of the most beautiful, free human being.

(You see, this is how I intoxicate myself for moments and forget the misery
of reality.)

Letter from Božena Němcová to Jan (Ivan) Helcelet, 29 July 1851. Iggers, Wilma. *Women of Prague*. Berghahn Books, 1995. 60.

Iggers' monograph includes her own extensive and excellent translations of Božena Němcová's correspondence, which appear throughout this book. Němcová's letters are startling and beautiful, and complicate and enhance every other claim about her. Jan (Ivan) Helcelet is one of Němcová's lovers, who appears again (and again) in this text.

Her Life

is from the very beginning shrouded in mystery—

"500 Czech Crown Banknote." *Prague.net.*

This is a short article about Němcová, whose image appears on the 500-crown banknote (approximately 25 U.S. dollars). Czech banknotes notably include several women: Agnes of Bohemia, Ema Destinnová, and Božena Němcová—a saint, an opera singer, and a writer.

It Could Not Be Otherwise

All the talented Czechs of the past century came from rather humble
circumstances—
it could not be otherwise—

and Božena Němcová, christened Barbora,
was the daughter of a Czech servant girl
and Johann Pankl, an Austrian *feschak* and horse groom

> who legitimized his newly born daughter after
> a brief delay.

Demetz, Peter. *Prague in Black and Gold*. Hill and Wang, 1998. 308.

This book's subtitle, "Scenes from the Life of a European City," echoes the subtitle
of *Babička*: "Scenes from Country Life." Demetz, who grew up in Prague but is now a
professor in the U.S., states his wish "to sketch a few selected chapters of a paradoxical
history in which the golden hues of proud power and creative glory, of emperors, artists,
and scholars, and restive people, are not untouched with the black of suffering and the
victims' silence" (xii). His book is historical but also personal, and full of his opinions. He
addresses theories about Němcová's origins but says that rather than focusing on who her
parents are, "it is far more important to grasp her pride and her thirst for independence,
her plea for women's education (she had almost none), her defense of Jews," and her
participation in the 1848 revolution (317).

Or

She was of high aristocratic origins:

the adventurous Duchess of Sagan
and
none other than Metternich, the imperial chancellor.

Demetz, *Prague in Black and Gold,* 308.

Princess Catherine Wilhelmine, Duchess of Sagan—known in Czech as Kateřina Zaháňská—lived at Ratibořice Castle, in the center of the village where Němcová was raised and the setting of several scenes in her novel *Babička.* There, the princess had an ongoing affair with Prince Klemens of Metternich, a married statesman and diplomat with close ties to Napoleon. Metternich eventually became Chancellor of the Austrian Empire. According to the *Wikipedia* entry on the princess, the affair began in 1813 when Metternich negotiated an "anti-Napoleonic coalition" at Ratibořice Castle, and is documented by over 600 letters that were discovered in 1949. Thus, some have suggested that Němcová could be their child, given over to the care of the princess' horse groomer, Johann Pankl, who suddenly married the fifteen-year-old Terezie Novotná.

Ratibořice Castle

We Don't Even Know

When she was born!   Not even the year!!
On her tombstone it says 1820 but her school records say 1818 or even further 1817!

And the mystery remains about her parents.

"500 Czech Crown Banknote," *Prague.net.*

Theory: Božena Němcová Was Goya's Granddaughter. What Do You Think?

The fate of our most famous writer is dramatic in itself, but there are new findings. Still many unanswered questions—perhaps not a mystery, but controversial moments.

Goya's fateful love affair with Doña Maria del Pilar Teresa Cayetana, the 13th Duchess of Alba, is well known. There are several etchings documented in Goya's estate: yet these prints appear many years later in the possession of Božena Němcová!

Mother unknown, unknown father?

Experts agree that the date of birth of Božena Němcová is 1816. That would be quite fitting, do not you think? But around 1816, Goya was seventy years old, lived in seclusion, and had trouble with the Inquisition. Fatherhood is not impossible but it is very questionable.

If not the daughter, why not the granddaughter?

Kočí, Jakub D. *"Teorie: Božena Němcová byla Goyova vnučka. Co vy na to?" Žena-in.* 7 Nov. 2013. (My translation with assistance from *Google Translate*.)

Published in a Czech online magazine for women (žena-in.cz), this article provides an interview with Františka Vrbenská and Petrem Vokáčem, who offer yet another theory about Němcová's origins: that Francisco Goya's affair with the Duchess of Alba produced an illegitimate daughter, Herminie, who then also, it appears, became the mother of an illegitimate daughter, who was put in foster care in Bohemia and named Barbora Panklová. The etchings mentioned above from Goya's estate, including one by Rembrandt, were apparently later found in Němcová's estate, and her grandson is said to believe the name Goya is encrypted into them. Was Goya Němcová's grandfather? Perhaps. But then again, a 2007 article by Elizabeth Nash in the UK's *Independent* claims that Goya's famous love story with the Duchess is nothing but an "urban legend."

It Should Be Mentioned Right Now

that much of the preceding is in doubt.

In any case, on with the story.

"Božena Němcová—*Babička.*" *Fortune City.*

This website was "last fussed over on 11/19/00" by an enthusiast of Franz Kafka, Milena Jesenská, and Božena Němcová.

Father

could get me to do anything
he knew me

spoke kindly, I would have

jumped in fire

for him, when he looked at me

beautiful blue

Letter from BN to unknown addressee, 1854. Iggers, *Women of Prague*, 64.

Iggers notes the recipient of the letter is an "unknown addressee," but since her book's publication in 1995, scholars have determined that the likely recipient was Hanuš Jurenka, with whom Němcová was having an affair at this time.

23

My Mother

was strict and spoke little to us children—she
ordered me do things   immediately

        punished me

for everything. I was always
supposed to ask her forgiveness
                        and thank her
                        for punishment.

I would not have done it even if she had killed me.

Letter from BN to unknown addressee (probably Hanuš Jurenka), 1854. Iggers, *Women of Prague*, 64.

Barunka Panklová

was badly treated by the woman until now presumed to be her mother. (Her attitude towards her daughter appeared to those around her more like a stepmother's than a mother's.)

Was this because she resented the illegitimate birth of her daughter, or because she was raising a child not her own?

And if Němcová was not Pankl's daughter, did she know it?

Iggers, *Women of Prague*, 49.

This is from Iggers' own introduction and commentary on Němcová.

The Twelve Months: The Unhappy Beginning

Once upon a time there was a mother who had two daughters—one was her own and the other one was her stepdaughter. The mother loved her own daughter very much but could not stand to look at her stepdaughter.

The reason was that Maruška was nicer than her own daughter Holena. But Maruška was not aware of her own beauty. That is why she could not understand why her stepmother wrinkled her forehead whenever she looked at her. Maruška thought perhaps that she did not comply with her mother's will.

When Holena adorned herself, rested in the room, and walked around the yard or in the street aimlessly, Maruška did all the housework—cleaned, cooked, washed, sewed, spun, carried hay home, and milked the cows. She did all the work, yet her stepmother cursed her every day.

It did not matter that she suffered like a martyr!
The situation grew worse and worse every day!

Němcová, Božena. "The Twelve Months." *Muzeum Boženy Němcové.*

This is one of many Slovak folk tales recorded by Němcová, and the museum website notes that, "This tale was told by Božena Němcová's servant Marka from Trenčianska." The name Maruška calls to mind Baruška, Němcová's own childhood nickname.

I Was Happy

When I go through the years of my life...I think...this can't be me!—

If you had known me when I was twelve, thirteen years old—I like to think about that time the most.

My body was already developed, but I was half maiden, half child. I was not embarrassed to climb on a tree in front of boys, or...to raise my skirts above my knees and to wade through the water, and to sit astride on a horse riding in the meadow—

I was happy about new shoes, clothes, and ribbons.

Letter from BN to unknown addressee (probably Jurenka), 1854. Iggers, *Women of Prague,* 64.

She Is the Wild Sort

There were some voices in the village which said:

"One must give the girl all honor as having skill and strength which no girl and very few men can equal. What girl can carry two buckets full of water and yet walk as if she were toying with them? And who can look after a herd as she can? A horse or bull, a cow or sheep, all obey her, she controls all of them. Such a girl is a real blessing in a household."

But if a youth here or there announced, "I'd like to make her my wife," the mothers at once shrieked, "No, no, my boy! Don't bring that girl into our family. No man can say how things will turn out with her. She is the wild sort—bewitched!"

Němcová, Božena. "Divá Bára." *Czechoslovak Stories*. Ed. and trans. Šárka B. Hrbková. Duffield, 1920. 172.

Written shortly after the publication of *Babička* in 1855, "Divá Bára" translates to "Wild Bára" or "Bewitched Bára." Though she is neither wild nor bewitched, the superstitious townfolk believe that Bára is a changeling replaced in her crib by the Noon Witch. (After giving birth, Bára's mother forgot that "a woman, after confinement, must never emerge from her room precisely at noon," leaving herself vulnerable to a visit from the Noon Witch.) Like Bára, Němcová had close friendships with women and was also ostracized by her various communities because she did not conform to their restrictive (even superstitious) ideas of what was acceptable for women.

Aren't You Truly Going to Think of Any of the Boys?

"No, no," Bára shook her head, smilingly. "I don't think of any of them, and when they come a-courting I make short work of them. Why should I spoil my thoughts, or bind up my golden freedom? I would rather tie a millstone around my neck and jump into the river."

Němcová, "Divá Bára," 172.

Ultimately even Bára falls for a strong and quiet huntsman. But first she saves her best friend Elška from an unhappy marriage by pretending to be the ghost that everyone thinks is haunting the town. She puts a sheet over herself and spooks the steward whom Elška seems doomed to marry, embarrassing him and successfully disrupting the nuptials. Bára's punishment is to spend the night alone in a cemetery vault, which she accepts bravely. Clips from the 1949 film with a beautiful, presumed-topless, hairy-armpitted woman strolling through the night woods can be found on *YouTube*.

"Divá Bára" is full of fascinating portrayals of gender roles and romantic relationships, all of which resolve in the happy heterosexual marriages promised at the end, but none of which are presented as problematic or shocking to the reader (even if they are to the fictional townspeople). When Bára is fifteen, "not a girl in the entire village could equal her in strength and size" and "strong boys were unable to conquer her in a fight." She is constantly having to defend her male friend Josífek from other boys, and the language of her relationship with her friend Elška is quite passionate: "In spirit she always embraced and kissed Elška for her friendship, though in reality she timidly refrained from expressing, as she longed to do, her fervent feeling" (167). Bára's first encounter with the huntsman, whom she will ultimately marry, took place when her two bulls locked horns, and he tried to intercede, but Bára was the one who succeeded in separating the bulls and protecting the huntsman.

Disproportionate Advantages

A number of Barunka's physical characteristics resembled the Duchess'. Barunka received, in comparison with her other siblings, disproportionate advantages.

Among these were her stay in Chvalkovice Castle for teaching, a home tutor who visited Barunka before she even started school, as well as the interest of the Duchess Zaháňská, who allowed her to borrow books from her castle library.

In short, the daughter of a coachman was receiving the unprecedented and extraordinary interest of nobility.

"Božena Němcová," *Radio Prague's Virtual Cemetery.*

Points of possible confusion include: that the Duchess is also interchangeably referred to as a Princess (both are correct) and that there are two castles in this passage. One is in Ratibořice, where Němcová grew up and where the Duchess Zaháňská lived and where key scenes from *Babička* are set. The other is in Chvalkovice, just a few miles away from Ratibořice, where Němcová received some tutoring. She otherwise did not have much formal education and therefore advocated for education, especially among rural villagers, much of her life.

In addition to two castles there are two sisters: While many have theorized that Duchess Kateřina Zaháňská is Němcová's mother, Czech historian Helena Sobková argues instead that Kateřina's sister Dorothea may in fact be her mother. Dorothea began a relationship with Count Jan Karel Clam-Martinic that ended abruptly in 1816, and Dorothea apparently disappeared from social life for nine months. In the meantime, the coachman of Ratibořice, Johann Pankl, who had previously signed a contract agreeing not to marry, found himself marrying Terezie Novatná in 1820, soon after the documented birth of a child. The documentation, however, disappeared when it was time to enroll their daughter in school.

Princess Kateřina Zaháňská / Božena Němcová

Princess Dorothea Talleyrand, sister of Kateřina / Božena Němcová

At Chvalkovice Castle

There I moved in a different circle
and my first naïve love stories began.

Letter from BN to unknown addressee (probably Jurenka), 1854. Iggers, *Women of Prague*, 64.

The Many-Layered Lady

Barunka's mother had her hands full and did not know what to do.

Her lively and imaginative seventeen-year-old daughter
described the life of the steward of Chvalkovice Castle

and his older wife with devastating precision:

> In the evening when she went to bed she rigged herself out like a
> wagoneer who wants to go to Amsterdam, with flannel drawers,
> a skirt, a bodice, stockings, a warm corset and a shawl around
> her neck.

The many-layered lady was jealous.

Demetz, *Prague in Black and Gold*, 309.

I Liked Most to Read

the history of Genoveva   and still dreamed
of bewitched princesses, about improbable deeds

and my favorite fantasy

*   was to enter a convent—*

just because I had heard
that nuns learn so much.

Letter from BN to unknown addressee (probably Jurenka), 1854. Iggers, *Women of Prague*, 64.

She Had No Patience with Poetry

she preferred   the admiring glances
of men   flirting   whispers   first kisses   long
hours reading   Schiller   Wieland   third-rate
German trash   nourishing dreams

      about a fairy-tale prince.

Demetz, *Prague in Black and Gold*, 309.

Demetz notes that Němcová hoped to improve upon her modest education and to refine her German. Only later would she appreciate and promote Czech language and culture.

This Pure, Beautiful Poetry

My beautiful youth, the sweet isolation in which I lived, the simple upbringing, in short

my ideal life as a girl, this pure, beautiful poetry—

> *You see only the prose of reality in it,*   *for me it remains a paradise.*

I still see every rock, every flower as they were when I was a girl full of imagination.

Letter from BN to her sister Adéla, 1856. Iggers, *Women of Prague*, 74.

Němcová was the oldest of twelve, six of whom survived infancy. Iggers notes that Adéla "seems to have been her favorite sibling." And Adéla is the name of Barunka's sister in *Babička*.

As Long As I Could Dance

Back then, when men used to stop and say, "That's a pretty girl!"
the words did not stay in my head.

To laugh, to dance, whether on the barn floor, in the servants' quarters,
in the meadow—

it didn't matter as long as I could dance!

Letter from BN to unknown addressee (probably Jurenka), 1854. Iggers, *Women of Prague*, 64.

Queen of the Dahlia Ball

A beautiful flower called dahlia has its origin in Mexico. Dahlia became a symbol of national revival and patriotism in Česká Skalice and its surroundings, and in 1836, Mr. Steidler built a magnificent hall in his inn which was made for annual autumn exhibitions of dahlias and at the same time for Dahlia Balls that were held on this occasion.

By a coincidence, the 1st Dahlia Ball took place two days

> after the wedding of Barunka Panklová and Josef Němec and they also took part of it.

Mrs. Němcová was crowned queen of the ball there.

"Steidler's Inn." *Muzeum Boženy Němcové.*

Built in 1824, Steidler's Inn has been the home of the Museum of Božena Němcová since 1962.

Queen of the Dahlia Ball

The Twelve Months: The Happy Ending

Maruška inherited the house, the cow, the small garden, and the field
and meadows around the house.

When spring came, a farmer had been found to manage the property.

A handsome lad, he soon wed good Maruška—
and they both lived well in peace and in love.

Němcová, "The Twelve Months."

The Happy Beginning

of this beautiful and talented girl's life would come to an end

in 1837   *when she was 17, or so, years old*
with her marriage to   *the 15-years-older*
Josef Němec   *who worked as a customs officer*

She had no hope of living free

absolute divergence of personalities

rough primitive man   inclinations to
brutality   despite patriotism
displays of courage could never win

        the love—

of intelligent delicate idealistic Božena Němcová.

At the same time he wasn't able
to get over loving her and give her

        up—because she was
        too beautiful.

And fascinating.

"Božena Němcová," *Radio Prague's Virtual Cemetery.* Italicized phrases from Němcová's *Wikipedia* entry.

The Very Beginning

Her marriage was a failure from the very beginning.

Bažant, Jan, Nina Bažantová, and Frances Starn, eds. "Defeated Politicians, Victorious Intellectuals." Introduction. *The Czech Reader: History, Politics, Culture*. Duke UP, 2010. 152.

When I Married, I Wept

for my lost freedom and the beautiful dreams and ideals of my life that were destroyed forever.

Letter from BN to unknown addressee (probably Jurenka), 1854. Iggers, *Women of Prague*, 64.

To Where Are They Leading the Maiden in the White Dress?

Why does her family lament her?—Are they perhaps going to burn her at the stake?—

Or perhaps in the temple the high priest waits with raised knife, to excise the fervent, vestal heart of the maiden, placing it as sacrifice onto the altar to a cold god?

Němcová, Božena. "Čtyry doby" ("The Four Seasons"). Trans. by Charles University Introduction to Czech Literature class. *Slovo a smysl*, or *Word & Sense: A Journal of Interdisciplinary Theory and Criticism in Czech Studies.* Vol. 1, 2004. 352.

This four-part narrative concludes with a dedication: "Written to my dear friend Josef Frič from Božena Němcová for New Year 1856." It was part of a collection dedicated to Frič, not intended for publication, and it was not published until thirty years after Němcová's death.

In an article from the same issue of *Word & Sense*, "Notes on 'the philosophy of love' in 'Four Seasons' by Božena Němcová," Jaromír Loužil explains that: "By dedicating 'Four Seasons' to the 'rebel' Josef Václav Frič, Němcová demonstrates her solidarity with the young generation, freer in its opinions and more advanced, and expresses the hope she places in it" (366).

Frič was a fellow writer and the "founder of Czech civic lyric poetry" whose verse "protested against autocratic oppression and glorified the revolutionary struggle of the Czech people in 1848." However, the online source used for Frič's biography, *The Free Dictionary*, cautions readers: "Warning! The following article is from *The Great Soviet Encyclopedia* (1979). It might be outdated or ideologically biased."

The Bride Does Not Listen

Beautifully the priest speaks of duties, of matrimonial faithfulness, of subservience, but the bride does not listen;

her soul dwells among the high rubber plants, at the feet of the sublime image, which preaches to her a sermon of divine, free love—

with which there is no need of promises or oaths!

Němcová, "Čtyry doby," 353.

Loužil further notes that, "in the radical version of her critique of marriage, Božena Němcová openly advocates 'free love,' which can be understood as a defense of open love [...]. True, i.e. free love, is incompatible with the institution of marriage" (360).

From the Bride He Requests an Oath

The priest has finished speaking.
From the bride he requests an oath, the oath

that she wants, with the man who holds her hand in his,
that she wants to go through life with him, to be with him for better,
for worse, until death.
That she wants patiently to endure whatever he might impose on her,

to deny herself at all times, voluntarily to become a slave!

Through the church resounds a dolorous 'I do'—and the gold band,
the inseparable band,
is turned around the hand of the bride.

—Oh bride, alas!

Němcová, "'Čtyry doby,'" 353.

In "'Čtyry doby' by Božena Němcová and 'Čtvero dob' by Tereza Nováková," Tereza Riedlbauchová describes this text as "a short story [...] which can even be read as four independent stories." She writes that Němcová "uses both a cyclical and parallel device, using her chapters to enforce the sense of parallel by repeating themes of church, for example, or nature. The cycle she uses is of seasons [...] as seasons of love in a woman's life" (62).

I Cried My First Bitter Tears

In the first eight days of my marriage
I cried my first bitter tears!

How beautiful I had imagined
life at the side of a man I loved.

I saw very early that our natures
were not suited for each other.

Letter from BN to her sister Adéla, 21 November 1856. Iggers, *Women of Prague*, 74.

What Have You Done in Ignorance!

You have sinned!—To another you have given your soul, to another your body, and the devil has folded you whole into his arms!

There is eating and drinking, singing and dancing, all for the happiness and prosperity of the husband and wife.

—The bride must come into the circle too!

Němcová, "Čtyry doby," 353.

Riedlbauchová notes that "the tragic third chapter starts with a wedding—though it is seen as a funeral or sacrifice. Both the narratives and motifs exploit contradictions such as a wedding as a betrayal of love" (62).

You Must, You Are Mine

A voice sounds in her ear: 'Come with me!'

A shiver runs down her, she forgets that she is ornamented with a crown of myrtle, and she says defiantly: 'I will not go!'

'You must, you are mine!' sounds the reply.

Němcová, "Čtyry doby," 353.

Critics have characterized this text as a a literary sketch with elements of the manifesto, a single story that can be read as four individual stories, a poem in prose, etc. Loužil says: "This genre ambiguity of 'Four Seasons' adds to its often repeated 'mysteriousness' and explains why the story is the subject of many new interpretations" (357).

Her Heart Hardly Beats

The bride kneels at the window. Behind her stands the bridal bed, the grinning face of the satyr draws back the curtains.—Is the bride listening to the music?—Is she praying?—Does her breast heave with desire?

She does not hear music, she does not pray, her heart hardly beats. The moon and stars shine wanly.

Němcová, "Čtyry doby," 353.

It Is Sad in the Garden!

The bride recollects the resplendent heavens, the May night!

She sees before her the enchantingly beautiful apparition, the nymphlike maiden smiles at her; but it is another's lip that inclines to her, into another's arms she involuntarily falls, and the apparition disappears.

In the morning at daybreak

she gets up from the bed a wan woman. Confusedly she looks around herself; she sees the virgin bed stained by the man who has remained alien to her soul, she sees the crumpled bridal gown, the withered wreath!

Němcová, "Čtyry doby," 353.

I Searched

for my ideal,
thinking that in the love for a man
I should find the completion
of myself.

Letter from BN to unknown addressee (probably Jurenka), 1854. Iggers, *Women of Prague*, 64.

Alone, and Always Alone

She must proceed alone, and always alone.

Despairingly she looks into the roaring waves.—'Would it not be better to cast myself into the cold current, to sate these desires in one stroke, to heal my burning pains and wounds?' she says to herself. 'Wherefore creep through life further?—For what?—Where is the goal of my journey?'

Němcová, "Čtyry doby," 354.

She Throws Herself into It

as though she wants to perish in the wild swirl,
as though she wants to escape from herself.

Němcová, "Čtyry doby," 353.

Shrouded in mystery

To where are they leading the maiden in the white dress?

A dolorous 'I do'

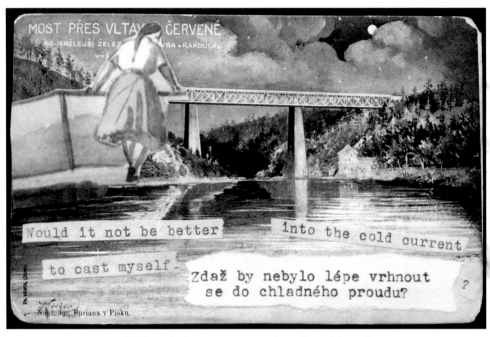

As though she wants to perish in the wild swirl

2. She Loved to Love

Exceedingly Complicated

Němcová, yearning for love and affection, in the end looked for the fulfillment of her dreams in extra-marital affairs.

Although these relationships were common for the society of the period, the writer was condemned during her love affairs by the public, because she failed to conceal them as much as others did.

In spite of the fact that, according to surviving accounts, Němcová was beautiful, witty, intelligent, and charming, her relations with men were exceedingly complicated.

"Božena Němcová," *Radio Prague's Virtual Cemetery.*

She Loved to Love

absolutely and in total disregard

and when as a married woman and caring mother of four

she chose a man
she abandoned herself

to her desires and letters almost blindly

her *grand amours*   recurrent depressing: *a night of nightingales*
a one-night stand on a Prague hill or newspaper office

then painful absence

renewed   embraces   confessions   correspondences

finally fiery
demands

on the men who usually feared   her
sudden passions   were unwilling

to become prisoners of her
almost
masochistic surrender.

Demetz, *Prague in Black and Gold*, 310–11.

One Lover's Sister

That fiery, desirable, perhaps even destructive woman...everything about her was charming.

She had many admirers and many women envied her and condemned her free behavior and the way she was celebrated among the literati.

Mrs. Němcová was very fearless. She went where nobody else dared to go. Living freely, without responsibility, she bore criticism with a smile.

Reminiscences of Anna Cardová-Lamblová, sister of Vilém Dušan Lambl, one of Němcová's lovers. Iggers, *Women of Prague*, 66.

In the years following her death, many of Němcová's contemporaries recorded reminiscences of their encounters with her, thus establishing her legacy as a celebrated figure of the national literary revival. The recollections from various sources were collected and published in 1927 in Zdeněk Záhoř's *Božena Němcová: Hlasy o osobnosti a o díle (Božena Němcová: Opinions of Her Life and Work)*. Iggers translates these reminiscences along with excerpts of Němcová's correspondence.

Němcová was often ill, and she developed intimate relationships with two of her doctors, Josef Čejka and Lambl, both of whom were active in the nationalist cause. She was introduced to Lambl in 1851 by her friends, the sisters Karolina Světlá and Žofie Podlipská.

Lambl was a physician who discovered an intestinal parasite that is now named after him: *Giardia lamblia*.

Božena Could Not Be Confined to the Roles of Wife and Mother

Her ebullient spirit took her into social circles
far beyond hearth and home.

Peaslee, Margaret H. "Božena Němcová Remembered." *Faculty Page.* U of Pittsburgh, Titusville.

Peaslee's faculty page can no longer be accessed because Peaslee passed away in 2016. The obituary of Margaret H. Peaslee, who was Professor Emerita of Biology, is illuminating. Her work on Gregor Mendel seemed to have led her to an interest in Mendel's mentor, František Matouš Klácel, which led her to Němcová, with whom Klácel was intimately connected. Peaslee's detailed obituary cites her Czech heritage and her enjoyment of "all things Czech, including researching Czech scientists and artists." Her final academic accomplishment was an October 2015 lecture on Klácel at the Czechoslovak Genealogical Society International Conference. She is now buried, along with Klácel, at the Bohemian National Cemetery in Chicago.

Her Daughter Dora

Wherever it was at all possible, mother kept poultry and other domestic animals.

She trained a little pig to walk from the courtyard up the steps to the porch and to the kitchen where we fed it. When it got a little bigger, it was sacrificed for a festive supper...after which mother sat down at the piano.

Mother was an excellent cook.

Early in the morning she used to go walking...in the dew...went swimming. And in the evening...drank Bavarian beer.

Reflections by BN's daughter, Theodora. Originally published in Záhoř, translated by Iggers, *Women of Prague*, 56.

Her Misfortune

She interacted with the movers and shakers of the time—
politicians, authors, educators, and journalists.
It was to her misfortune, however, that she

unsuccessfully searched for love and
a soul mate within—

this circle of her friends.

Peaslee, "Božena Němcová Remembered."

Her Lovers

Today, four great loves are known to have gone on for more than 10 years altogether.

"Božena Němcová," *Radio Prague's Virtual Cemetery.*

It is unclear which four great loves are being referred to.

One Might Say Her Succession of Lovers

Němcová is known to have had relationships with Václav Bolemír Nebeský, Josef Čejka, Vilém Dušan Lambl, Ignác Jan Hanuš, Jan (Ivan) Helcelet, Hanuš Jurenka, František Matouš Klácel, and perhaps others.

Iggers, *Women of Prague*, 50; footnote, 87.

All of these men were intellectuals affiliated with the nationalist cause.

Václav Bolemír Nebeský

Odvážím se, ač i váhá ruka—
Roušku sejmu z dávno zašlé doby,
Otevru mechem porostlé hroby,
Vzkřisím mrtvé slasti, stará muka,
Zotvírám své duše všechny brány
A odkryju srdce svého rány.—

I dare, though with a hesitant hand—
To remove the veil of bygone times,
Open the mossy graves,
I resurrect dead pleasures, old anguish,
All gates of the faithful soul
Reveal the heart of the wounds.—

Poem by Václav Bolemír Nebeský. Záhoř, Zdeněk, Ed. *Výbor z korespondence Boženy Němcové*. Stanislav Minařík, 1922.

Excerpt of a poem written by Václav Bolemír Nebeský, dedicated to Němcová in 1851, and published in the opening pages of her correspondence. Translation is my own, with help from *Google Translate*. These lines have an abbacc rhyme scheme that I did not attempt to duplicate.

Nebeský edited Němcová's first poem, "Ženám českým" ("To Czech Women"), and the two became close. He left to study in Vienna and grew jealous when Němcová began spending time with her doctor, Josef Čejka. This poem was written years after their relationship, when Nebeský was still clearly pained by the recollection.

Ignác Jan Hanuš

You have never seen such an objective female

when you see her you'll go totally crazy over her. She has experienced some tough times in her life and enough troubles, coarseness too in part, but she has still preserved her refined body and soul.

Too bad she does not have a different husband, or rather,

it would be better if she did not have one at all.

Letter from Ignác Jan Hanuš to a friend. Originally published in Záhoř, translated by Iggers, *Women of Prague*, 60.

Němcová became quite close with Hanuš, who was one of the central figures in the brotherhood established by František Matouš Klácel.

Father František Matouš Klácel

I consider the greatest treasure in my miserable life the favor of this Božena. We have been corresponding for a long time...our letters have been becoming ever more fervent, the kind of letters which will one day become common among mankind.

We have brought back the poetry which had escaped from the world.

Letter from František Matouš Klácel to Vojtěch Náprstek in 1851. Translated by Iggers, *Women of Prague*, 59.

Klácel was the founding member of the "brotherhood" that included Jan Helcelet, Ignác Hanuš, Němcová, and her husband Josef Němec. Klácel wrote a series of "Letters from a friend to a female friend on the origin of socialism and communism" (1849) addressed to Němcová under the pseudonym Ludmila. Though written "from a friend to a friend," it is apparently clear that he wished for more from their relationship. One idea he shared with her in a letter was: "Cast aside marriage as an unjust establishment, which enslaves and gives the body over in exclusive ownership to another person."

Vojtěch Náprstek, the letter's recipient, was a prominent figure and an advocate for women. He was christened with the (awesome) German name Adalbert Fingerhut, but, in the tradition of many nationalists including Němcová, later changed it to the Czech version of the name. He secretly left Prague for Milwaukee in 1848 after the uprisings, and returned ten years later. Němcová frequently wrote to him with requests for money.

Jan (Ivan) Helcelet

Keep well, my Ivan! I could easily slip into romantic thoughts.

The moon shines with a full face into my windows, the fragrance blows pleasantly into my room, all around is silence, there is nothing lacking but the sound of a stage coach stopping under the windows.

Kisses from your B.

Letter from BN to Jan (Ivan) Helcelet. 29 July 1851. Iggers, *Women of Prague*, 60.

Ivan is an alternate form of Jan.

A Memorable Night

From fairly delicate remarks in various letters it is clear that she and Helcelet spent a memorable night together, and that the next morning Father Klácel's eyes were red from crying.

Iggers, *Women of Prague*, 62.

So Many Thousand Thoughts Run to You

You are always on my mind. The days run like waves, as many drops of water as there are in a wave, so many thousand thoughts run to you, dear Ivan!

There was a time when I was indifferent to dying, but now I wish to see the children somewhat independent.

I would like to work for the dawn of a better future!

Letter from BN to Helcelet. 29 July 1851. Iggers, *Women of Prague*, 60.

The Sort of Lovers

The insipid and verbose letter Helcelet wrote to Němcová terminating their affair does still exist, and I am including parts of it to illustrate the sort of lovers Němcová encountered.

Iggers, *Women of Prague*, 87.

It Is Not Your Relationship with Your Husband That Bothers Me

although I suspect that that would happen in time.

What are unbearable to me are the dissonances
which come from my close connection with Hanuš,
and from your and my relationship with Matouš,
and from my inability to swim without harm

in this whirlpool of lies and pretenses.

Letter from Helcelet to BN, undated, referring to Ignác Hanuš and F. Matouš Klácel,
members of the brotherhood. Footnoted in Iggers, *Women of Prague*, 88.

I Announce to You

that I have decided to stop our correspondence.

Shrug your shoulders about my brains, make faces about my clumsiness,
but leave alone the bitterness for which you would have cause.

But even if you should feel more bitter
about the matter than I want you to be, I want you to know that

>   *nothing*

Letter from Helcelet to BN, undated. Iggers, *Women of Prague*, 88.

Again and Again, Bitterness

All these men belonged to patriotic circles or were well-educated medical students or doctors, but none had the courage to confront her expectations, and what remained to her was, again and again, bitterness, silence, and despair.

Demetz, *Prague in Black and Gold*, 311.

I Could Have Easily Gotten Over Losing His Body

for sexual feeling alone was never my motive for loving,
but his lack of trust always insulted me most painfully.

For his sake, I wish his wife remains as faithful to him
as I was.

If he wants to speak to me, talk him out of it.
But if we should see each other, I am afraid he would either repel me
or I would have to love him again, and I don't want either.

If I could at least have fulfilled the longing of your heart,
I would have undertaken anything, but those were vain hopes.

...this is my first and last such letter, in the future I shall only write to you
about sensible things.

Letter from BN to Václav Bendl, whom Iggers calls "a student and poet much younger than herself," 14 December 1856. Iggers, *Women of Prague,* 77. Here Němcová is discussing with Bendl her relationship with Hanuš Jurenka, who is Bendl's friend.

In another letter from 1856, Němcová tells Bendl of a dream she has in which Jurenka set his head on her lap while Bendl "smoked and told jokes." She recounts that in the dream she suggested that Bendl "make an impromptu poem on our situation," at which point Bendl "began a very humorous improvisation in a pathetic tone about us as a three-leaf clover" (Iggers 77).

The three-leaf clover image can apply to other "love triangles" in which men became rivals for Němcová's affections. First was the rivalry between Nebeský and Čejka. Then Helcelet and Klácel. Now Bendl and Jurenka.

Bendl had already written her a poem a year earlier (excerpted on the next page). She is said to have had an affair with Bendl, and this letter hints at their intimacy (*"If I could at least have fulfilled the longing of your heart"*).

Václav Bendl

Podivná ty ženo! chladná—žhavá—
Kdo se dívá v to tvé duchaplné oko
V němž tu sálá žár, tu slast dlí hravá,
Může nepovznést se s tebou k hvězdám převysoko?

You strange woman! Cold—hot—
He who gazes at your clever eye,
Here radiates heat, here dwells playful delight,
May he rise with you high up to the stars?

Poem by Václav Bendl. Záhoř, *Výbor z korespondence Boženy Němcové*.

This is my translation of the first stanza of a poem written by Bendl in 1855 and dedicated to Němcová. It is published on the opening page of her collected correspondence.

Her Husband Certainly Knew Something

of Božena's passionate affairs

evidence he crudely mistreated her
            or locked her up in her room

                                    (she had to—escape
                                    through the window)

Marital rape has a variety of methods.

Demetz, *Prague in Black and Gold,* 310.

That Marital Duty

is the foundation of everything for him and he cannot get it either by threats or begging. For a person like him it is of course terrible, and I am surprised he likes me...and so God knows how things would be between us if there were no separations.

Perhaps when he is again employed he will go back to his old routine, and no longer having me before his eyes, he will do what he did earlier, and time will perhaps wipe out my insurmountable revulsion which keeps me from obeying what the priests command.

And yet I would sometimes like to sacrifice in that temple of Venus.

Letter from BN to Helcelet. 18–19 June 1856. Iggers, *Women of Prague*, 69.

Oh I Sometimes Long for It Very Much

and I have to muster my whole strength to overcome myself, but you know that to have human feelings is considered a sin. Hanuš of course does not believe it, to him it seems incomprehensible that I, having enough opportunities, should not enjoy what the body desires and is part of a complete life, either with my husband or with anybody else. And yet it has been so—for more than a year...I only loosened my reins last year, without it all having a deeper substance, and experienced enough from poisonous mouths.

—At any rate, I don't know a single man to whom I would dare say: "Grant me delicious moments in your arms!" Each would say to me: "Go, sinful Magdalene."

I think you would also hold it against me, as against any woman.

Letter from BN to Helcelet. 18–19 June 1856. Iggers, *Women of Prague*, 69.

A Delightful Sin

It is perhaps one of my good qualities that I am somewhat sensitive to everything beautiful; but what is even greater is my sensitivity to everything that disturbs, insults beauty, and therefore sins against it. Don't think I want to atone...for a delightful sin.

In my belief a beautiful sin has its moral dignity and merit—what is not beautiful about it contains its own punishment.

Letter from Jan Helcelet to BN, undated. Iggers, *Women of Prague*, 88.

What I Wanted

was to take you in my arms, press my lips on yours,
and hear your words in the depth of your sensitive soul.

My dear one! You're my most passionate, my only love.
Without you I feel sad and anxious.

Letter from Žofie Rottová Podlipská to BN during Němcová's three-month stay in Ďarmoty in 1852. Quoted in Frančíková, Dagmar. "All Czechs, but Particularly Women: The Positionality of Women in the Construction of the Modern Czech Nation, 1820s–1850s." Dissertation. University of Michigan, 2011. 64.

Noting their use of passionate language, Frančíková calls the three-year relationship between these two women a "romantic friendship." Frančíková provides a thorough examination of the nature of the letters exchanged between Czech women nationalists, particularly Němcová's with other women, and concludes that, "Although Czech scholars frequently enjoy speculating about the number of extramarital heterosexual affairs that this legendary Czech author had, it is possible that her same-sex sexual relationships and desires might potentially be an issue that could seriously endanger the carefully crafted image of the 'pledge and shield of this country'" (96).

What I wanted

Believe Me

Sometimes I dream that your eyes are here right in front of me,

                         I am drowning in them,

and they have the same sweet expression as they did when they used to ask:

       Božena, what's wrong?
       Božena, I love you.

Letter from BN to Žofie Rottová Podlipská, 1853. Quoted in Frančíková, "All Czechs," 64.

Frančíková provides an excellent overview of friendships between women in the context of contemporary advice books, which encourage female friendships as a means of support for the heterosexual marriage and family unit. But Frančíková notes that in another letter Němcová "shared a recent dream in which Rottová was getting married and (despite the fact that Němcová herself had been married) both women were devastated that her marriage caused her to leave Němcová" (76).

This echoes a passage in "Divá Bára" when, as the close friends Bára and Elška cast St. John's wreaths into the stream (a ritual in which the wreath is believed to float toward one's prospective husband), the girls promise one another, after silence and a blush, that if one doesn't marry, the other won't marry either.

How Men Judge

What seemed beautiful, ideal a few years ago, I now see as artificial empty form, so that I wonder how I could ever have considered it anything else.

I won't repeat to you how men judge my personality, they normally lie to us and sometimes make us into angels and sometimes into devils.

Letter from BN to Veronika Vrbíková, 22 Jan 1851. Iggers, *Women of Prague*, 58.

Němcová frequently addressed her friend Vrbíková as "sister," which Frančíková suggests is a reflection of both a friendship on par with a familial bond and of the women's sense of "sisterhood," their shared pursuit of the nationalist cause.

I Myself Sometimes Consider Myself the Worst in This World

I don't feel free anywhere this year,   clouds everywhere, everywhere.

*I see the sword of Damocles above me.   As if there was not enough
unhappiness, the doctor tells me he won't recover.   I also hear such
unpleasant reports   ruining my reputation   that I don't even
know how I'll show my face in Prague.   I would like best not to
return until*
           all have forgotten that I was ever in the world.

                              If only that child would get better!

*If I had money and if Hynek were well, I would emigrate with the
children far away, perhaps to America.*

*Love me and be convinced that Božena is not as bad as that gang makes
her out to be.*
And you loved me even with my faults.

           I myself sometimes consider myself the worst in this world.

Letter from BN to Karolina Světlá, 30 August 1853. Iggers, *Women of Prague*, 63.

Němcová was right to express these concerns, but perhaps she was wrong in believing Světlá loved her even with her faults. Světlá was a fellow writer who "broke with Němcová over her lifestyle." Světlá is the sister of Žofie Rottová Podlipská, with whom Němcová exchanged passionate letters. This letter apparently refers specifically to Němcová's parting with Lambl.

In "Social chronicler and society girl Karolina Světlá," a 2007 article for *Radio Prague*, Tomas Edel discusses the relationship between Světlá and Němcová: "We know for sure, because Světlá writes it in her memoirs, that she got really annoyed with Němcová when she lent her some money, and right in front of Světlá's eyes, Němcová handed a sum of this money straight over to one of her lovers. This really got modest and economical Světlá's back up."

The moon shines with a full face

My miserable life

The Brotherhood

VÁCLAV ČENĚK BENDL

Podivná ty ženo!

Chladná – žhavá –

Kdo se diví v to tvé duchaplné oko,

v němž tu sálá žár, tu slast dít bravá,

může nepozorait se s tebou k hvězdám přenysoko?

Při tobě, při tom ocean vroucích citů,

kdož může chladným, prázdným srdcem rozhodnosti,

zda před tebou se vzdálit věčně do skrytu,

zda ti na věže věky nutno uniknouti,

či roztoužený žáře prudkost, a raděj nocí,

po tobě toužit; před tebou se na prach bortit,

zda láskou, či snad ještě bozoumnějši

k tobě lnouti!

He who gazes

94

Clouds everywhere, everywhere

3. A Way of Life

The Little Stars of Gold, Part Two

"God bless it to you."

By this time it was quite dark. Going a little further on in the wood, Božena met another little girl, shivering with the cold. She had no shirt. She

seemed to be in great distress. This excited Božena's pity. "I'll give her my shawl. I am sure that I can spare it," she said to herself, as she parted with it. A short ways farther on, she met another little girl, so poor that she had

no skirt. It was already towards the end of autumn and winter was coming on. Božena took off her own skirt and gave it to the poor little girl. The cold did not trouble Božena so very much, as she knew that she had done

a good deed, and her little heart grew warm at the thought of it.

Němcová, "Little Stars of Gold."

The Human Heart

—Oh, who could plumb the depths of this unfathomable ocean with its cliffs and pits, its rich treasures, terrible monsters, this ocean called the human heart!

Letter from BN to sister Adéla, 3 June 1857. Iggers, *Women of Prague*, 75.

A Very Wonderful Moral Side

In addition to her other mental qualities, Němcová had a very wonderful moral side which was disastrous for her under the given circumstances—with her absolute generosity she was as trusting as a child.

She gave without hesitation.

For weeks she housed unknown girls from the country, who pretended an irresistible longing for education but had totally different interests.

Young men also were not ashamed to ask Němcová for money for trips to the country.

Božena sometimes gave all she had in her purse.

Karolina Světlá quoted in Iggers, *Women of Prague*, 57.

Iggers notes that Světlá thought Němcová was "not very hard working" and referenced Němcová's education ("she had after all only been educated in a village school"), implying that Němcová's literary friends wrote her works (58). As a major writer herself, Světlá was in a unique position in terms of shaping Němcová's legacy, and generally seems to have opted to focus on the positive. This passage, which reflects the friendship and tension between these women, originally appeared in Světlá's memoir, *Z literárního soukromí* (*From a Private Literary Life*), published in 1880, nearly two decades after Němcová's death.

They Also Held It Against Her

that she wrote so many letters, that she spent a guilder a month for postage! They gossiped about her a lot.

Reminiscences of Kateřina Emlerová-Dlabačová regarding the opinions held by the "ladies of Nymburk." Originally published in Záhoř, translated by Iggers, *Women of Prague*, 55.

Nymburk is a town outside of Prague where Němcová and her husband moved following the 1848 revolution when she and her husband were put under police surveillance.

of this passionate and beautiful woman whose sudden appearance out of the provinces a few generations before our own time had created a sensation among the patriots and the Czech language zealots in Prague.

Brod, Max. *Franz Kafka: A Biography*. Schocken, 1960. 251.

Franz Kafka was born in Prague in 1883, twenty-one years after Němcová's death. Kafka's family was both Jewish and German-speaking, which made him an outsider in the Czech capital. He grew up reading Němcová's writings.

Things Which Aroused Kafka's Understanding

Her unhappy marriage,
her burning love affairs with fellow nationalists,
her tender care for her children,
her raptures and depressions,
her tempestuous life which contrasted so strongly
with her somewhat old-fashioned manner of
writing,
her early death

—all these were things which aroused Kafka's understanding and
sympathy, with which he could well identify.

Brod, *Franz Kafka: A Biography*, 251–52.

Kafka and Max Brod met in 1902 when they were both students at Charles University, and they became good friends and literary allies. When Kafka died in 1924, Brod was the executor of Kafka's will, which included instructions to burn all of Kafka's writings. Brod famously opted to publish rather than burn Kafka's writings. As Brod says in the first edition of Kafka's *The Trial:* "Franz should have appointed another executor if he had been absolutely and finally determined that his instructions should stand."

Letter from Kafka to Milena Jesenská

But in any case: That's no ordinary writer who wrote this. Having read it I have almost as much confidence in your writing as I have in you as a person. I know in Czech (with my limited knowledge) only one music of language, that of Božena Němcová, here is another music, but related to the former in determination, passion, loveliness and above all a clairvoyant intelligence.

Kafka, Franz. *Letters to Milena*. Ed. Willy Haas. Trans. Tania and James Stern. Schocken, 1953. 35.

Milena Jesenská was an early translator of Kafka's writing from German to Czech who became one of his major love interests. They exchanged letters from 1920 to 1923—she writing in Czech, he responding in German.

Her Letters

He frequently read aloud to me from her letters, which so far as I know have not been translated out of the Czech, although they belong among the great documents of a struggling soul.

Brod, *Franz Kafka: A Biography*, 252.

Brod is referring to Kafka, who read Němcová's letters to him. With the exception of Iggers' select translations, Němcová's letters remain untranslated into English.

were essential not only to maintain contact with people she loved, but also to preserve her identity in very depressing living conditions. She had to tell her thoughts to somebody, and share her recollections, fears and hopes. She had to enforce a claim to a life of her own not only as a Czech patriot in a German-dominated society, but also as a woman writer in a world totally governed by men.

Bažant, et al., *The Czech Reader*, 152.

Letter to Her Husband

*I had more than one admirer—one had a mind, the other a body, that one
a heart, another intelligence, but in the end I never found what I longed for:*

    a man to whom I would gladly subject myself.
    —All had their weaknesses.

               I would choose none of them for a husband.

Letter from BN to her husband Josef Němec, 13 June 1857. Iggers, *Women of Prague*, 80.

Letter to Her Sister

Marriage is like an inflated pillow.
Once there is even the smallest tear in it, all the air escapes.
The lazy, heavy body remains.

Letter from BN to sister Adéla, 21 November 1856. Iggers, *Women of Prague*, 75.

They Married without Love

Mr. Němec was basically not a bad man, but he was not right for Mrs. Němcová. She was so gentle, calm, kind, and sweet as a dove and he, Mr. Commissar, was rash, stubborn, somber, materialistic...
they married without love.

Reminiscences of Marie Langhammerová, BN's former maid. Originally published in Záhoř, translated by Iggers, *Women of Prague*, 68.

Her Husband

He was tall, far beyond the usual height, had a swarthy face, severe features, his hair and eyes were black, and he spoke very loudly. He was good-hearted and sharp as flint.

Overall, he made a favorable impression. He was an honorable man, and for his circumstances was well educated. It was said of him that he was "ultra" Czech. He was very proud of his wife and enjoyed her literary work.

Quote from Žofie Podlipská, transcribed from a display at the Muzeum Boženy Němcové.

He Did Not Wish His Wife To Be a Writer

        wanting her

to be a devoted and practical housewife
as were the other petit bourgeois
women of Prague.

Demetz, *Prague in Black and Gold*, 310.

The Important Thing Is That She Was a Writer

which was in her times quite unusual—woman and a writer. Back then writers were just among men. Using today's words we would call her a feminist.

She was breaking the ice also by trying to earn her living with her writing skills only which was, again, very bizarre.

"500 Czech Crown Banknote," *Prague.net*.

Němcová spent her final years begging for money and surely never would have imagined her own image on Czech currency.

A Way of Life

She herself regarded her writing as a service to her nation; later however, her writing increasingly became a way of life, a means of living and a source of independence—the only possible material and spiritual survival available to a creative woman.

Šmejkalová, Jiřina. "Božena Němcová." *Biographical Dictionary of Women's Movements and Feminisms in Central, Eastern, and South Eastern Europe.* Eds. Francisca de Haan, Krassimira Daskalová, and Anna Loutfi. Central European UP, 2006. 369.

The Love She Was Missing

in her life

was at least deposited

in her stories, fairy tales, and novels.

"Božena Němcová," *Radio Prague's Virtual Cemetery.*

Fairy Tales

If you think of the tales of mysterious forests, wicked witches, and virtuous peasants, you probably think of the Brothers Grimm. But there is another reviver of fairy tales, little known in the West, who is deeply intriguing.

Božena Němcová was a feminist, revolutionary, and writer who collected fairy tales and folklore from the Bohemian countryside.

But for all she is a heroine nowadays, in her own lifetime she was much reviled, since she flouted both literary and social conventions—she was too much of a tearaway and a rebel, so was sidelined out of public life.

Callow, John. "Sorceress of the Folk Spirits: Božena Němcová." From the online abstract of a talk given by Dr. John Callow in 2008 at Treadwell's Books in London.

Barbora Němcová Changed Her Name to Božena

This openly referred to the Old Czech Legend about a peasant girl Božena whom a prince took for his wife.

Source unknown.

The Old Czech legend mentioned here is "Oldřich and Božena," which was translated into English in the 1832 *Cheskian Anthology: Being a History of the Poetical Literature of Bohemia with translated specimens* by John Bowring.

Many Families Named Their Girls Božena

My mother used to tell us that when she went walking in the fields she often met Němcová...with field flowers in her hands, in her waist, and in her hair. She used to say that she never met a more beautiful woman.

When the name of Božena Němcová appeared in Czech literature...many families named their girls Božena.

The name of the famous writer always lived in honor and love.

Reminscences of Vlasta Pitternová, "daughter of a minor patriot." Iggers, *Women of Prague*, 52.

Němcová Followed Her Husband

to Southwestern Bohemia, a region famous for its folklore tradition. She arrived full of enthusiasm. For her, ethnographical field-work was a mission, literary as well as patriotic. Her rural background and her natural ease in making social contacts won her the confidence of the notoriously distrustful Czech peasant.

Součková, Milada. *The Czech Romantics*. Mouton, 1958. 139.

I am a Stranger

I grew up as a free child of nature;
I am a stranger to the details of etiquette,
and nothing is easier for me
than to make a social blunder here and there.

Němcová, quoted in Součková, *The Czech Romantics*, 139.

And the Country Folk!

The people here are frighteningly backward. They speak Czech because they do not know German, but they know beans about higher education and national feeling. And the country folk! In one village a stone mason teaches school, elsewhere it is a cabinet maker who doesn't know how to read properly, and if he wants the children to write, he has to first have someone write it out for him. One could cry bloody tears.

How many talents, how many a clever head will perish before achieving the right consciousness!

Very few know anything about history, or have ever read a book; they come to me from the villages where I am known to lend books and they read at night in spinning circles.

Those rural people are my joy. I always perk up when a peasant woman extends her calloused hand and asks warmly: "Why haven't you come to see us for so long?"

Letter from BN to Bohuslava Čelakovská-Rajská, one of the foremost educators of Czech girls. 14 Feb 1846. Iggers, *Women of Prague*, 53.

According to Frančíková, who discusses Němcová's correspondence with other women: "Němcová also corresponded with Rajská whom she knew from the women's meetings, and their relationship had a very different character than that Němcová formed with Rottová. Němcová and Rajská became especially close in 1844 when Němcová provided her friend with advice regarding a difficult decision which led Rajská to accept František Ladislav Čelakovský's marriage offer" (75-76).

Pozdrav z Lečic p. Řípem.

And the country folk!

I Remember Her Well

I was then a young girl, but I remember her well. She liked to go to the villages, talked to the people and listened to them. Once she came to our farm for milk, but nobody knew her. She wore a little hat with ribbons and flowers. Her hair was parted in the middle. With her was a lady from town. When they wanted to go home, it began to rain. They were afraid that their hats would get wet and asked to leave them with us.

One day those ladies came again and asked for their hats...and out of one the blind heads of kittens were looking. We all laughed, and that Mrs. Němcová as well. We took the kittens out and the ladies went home.

We only found out later that it was Němcová, the writer of those beautiful sayings.

Reminiscences of Mrs. Podestátová, a "peasant woman from around Domažlice." Originally published in Záhoř, translated by Iggers, *Women of Prague*, 54–55.

One Evening

When she was spending the night on a friend's estate, she listened from her bedroom to the songs of country lovers wooing.

Součková, *The Czech Romantics,* 134.

Pictures from Slovakian Life

While traveling in Slovakia, she passed through a countryside as rustic as a romantic artist could desire. Němcová would browse through old parish documents or—on the spur of the moment—watch shepherds making regional cheese.

All of a sudden the report would change into a brilliant portrayal of the men of the Detva region—a portrayal of living epic heroes, of their stature, garments, habits, songs, and heroic deeds.

She was the first modern Czech artist to reveal the beauty of the Carpathian mountains and to write about the men who live in the primeval beech forests and fight the bear.

Součková, *The Czech Romantics,* 134–135.

Pictures from Slovakian life

The Bliss of the Dance

If you want to see real joy you have to see the peasant dance. The farmer may be harassed by all kinds of worries, but when he is dancing he forgets all his miseries and lives entirely for the bliss of the dance. Should death itself look over his shoulder, he would dance with gusto to the very end.

Young, old, married, single, everyone dances; everyone would sacrifice sleep, health, and even life itself in favor of the dance.

Němcová, quoted in Součková, *The Czech Romantics*, 140–141.

From 1845–1848, Němcová wrote a number of "Sketches from Domažlice," which Součková translates and summarizes. These ethnographic portraits of country life in Bohemia were considered part of her literary contribution to the nationalist revival.

lking Bird, the Living Water, and the Golden Apple - Tree

Jakob Malý publicly claimed that one of Božena Němcová's fairy tales was not an Authentic Czech Fairy Tale because it was too similar to "Story of the Two Sisters" from *The Arabian Nights*.

He was nonetheless a very poor writer.

She answered in the magazine *Květy* in a rather brusque manner, offering to take the critic to the woman who had been her informant for the controversial tale.

Malý answered politely that he had never intended to accuse Němcová of literary forgery.

The entire problem of 'authenticity' was distasteful to Němcová.

Součková, *The Czech Romantics*, 133–134.

The first paragraph is paraphrased.

When I Hear a Fairy Tale All Twisted

I have to write an introduction for the fourth part of my fairy tales, and I have to say what is mine and what is national; I will do it, but not with pleasure, for I will have to confess that many a tale was not national, and I know beforehand that this will be held against me.

When I hear a fairy tale all twisted and confused, I cannot resist making changes.

In some places I add and in others I delete, especially the ugly parts.

BN in a letter to an unknown addressee in February 1846. Quoted in Součková, *The Czech Romantics*, 134.

A Tale Without End

Once upon a time, about sunset, a little shepherd lad was pasturing his sheep, near a wide brook. Of course the boy was in a great hurry to get home, where he knew a good supper was waiting for him.

Now the wide brook had only a narrow plank for a bridge, so that the sheep were obliged to cross over, in a line, one at a time.

Now children, let us wait till the boy has driven all his sheep over the bridge, then I will finish my story.

Němcová, Božena. "A Tale Without End." *The Disobedient Kids and Other Czecho-Slovak Fairy Tales.* Trans. William H. Tolman and V. Smetanka. Koči, 1921. 2–3.

This is the entire tale.

So many letters

131

Kafka

Mr. Husband

Crowns

4. A Mode of Remembering

Her Son Hynek

Hynek has been in Prague since the holidays, in the Czech main school at Amerlinger. He learns very well; there are good teachers and teaching; as well as ordinary classes, they have biology, history, geography, physics, chemistry, geometry, drawing, singing, and gymnastics.

Letter from BN to Josef Myška, 28 January 1850. Transcribed from a display at the Muzeum Boženy Němcové.

137

Her Gifted Son Hynek

their young son Hynek

        our oldest son Hynek

her beloved oldest son Hynek

her favorite son Hynek

                her beloved son, Hynek

Various sources.

That Child

As if there was not enough unhappiness,

                    the doctor tells me he won't recover.

          If only that child would get better!

If I had money and if Hynek were well—

Letter from BN to Karolina Světlá, 30 August 1853. Iggers, *Women of Prague*, 63.

The following pages are an erasure of this letter.

If Hynek

                                        enough unhappiness

        he won't

                                                        If only

                if Hynek

He Won't

                                                          enough

                        he won't

                                   Hynek

Hynek

Hynek

Her Gifted Son Hynek

      died   of consumption at the age of 15

            —and still worse, their young son Hynek   died

and then 19 October our oldest son Hynek   died . . .

Shortly after the death   of her beloved oldest son Hynek in 1853,
she began work

After the death   of her favorite son Hynek in 1853, she
started writing *Babička*

She wrote it after the death   of her beloved son, Hynek.

Various sources.

In her detailed discussion of the relationship between public health (especially women's health) and the Czech nationalist movement, Frančíková notes that, "Even a cursory look at contemporary correspondence and journals shows that consumption was a rather common occurrence [...]. Němcová's correspondence provides another interesting account of people including her own son who were sick, and died, of consumption" (159–160).

After Hynek's Death

I found the slip of paper where I had written the plan for The Grandmother *three years ago.*

I read it   with increasing pleasure,   and as a mirage the charming picture of the little valley
                    arose before me, and in it the quiet household
                              where the grandmother was the main person.

                    How that memory consoled me,

          carrying me   from the grief of life

to the pleasant days of youth.

                              I eagerly began working.

Letter from BN to Helcelet, 4 June 1855. Iggers, *Women of Prague*, 67.

Her Best Known and Widely Read Book

Babička, in English *Grandmother*, was published in 1855. It is a book about her childhood and her happy memories of her kind and wise maternal grandmother, Magdalena Novotná. The simple, almost saintly Grandmother who comes to live with her daughter and grandchildren.

She lives on as the true incarnation of Czech folk wisdom and kindness, forever surrounded by sublime forests and green meadows.

First paragraph from "500 Czech Crown Banknote," *Prague.net*; second from Demetz, *Prague in Black and Gold*, 309.

The Old Lady Is a Perpetual Comfort

It is anything but a coincidence that when Sixty-Eight Publishers, the Toronto-based émigré publishing house run by Josef Škvorecký and his wife Zdena Salivarová during the years of normalization, published its hundredth book, it was not a smuggled *samizdat* manuscript by Ludvík Vaculík, Ivan Klíma, or Václav Havel, but a celebratory reprint of *Granny*.

The old lady is a perpetual comfort in times of trouble.

Sayer, Derek. *Prague, Capital of the Twentieth Century: A Surrealist History*. Princeton UP, 2013. 188.

After the Prague Spring of 1968, which ended with Soviet tanks rolling into Prague, a period of "normalization"—the restoration of Soviet rule in Czechoslovakia—began. Although the Soviets approved of Němcová because of her socialist tendencies, the Czechs embraced her nationalist celebration of Czech language and culture.

Phrases such as "the old lady" are typical of the tone of Sayer's conversational, 450-page "Surrealist History" of Prague. Earlier he refers to Josef Sudek, who famously photographed the renovation of Prague Castle in the early twentieth century, as the "one-armed photographer" (37). He later clarifies that Sudek "left his other arm in Italy" (40), the result of friendly fire in WWI.

Our Grandmother

is no more; for many a year now she has slept beneath the cold earth.

But to me she is not dead. Her image, with its lights and shadows, is imprinted upon my soul, and, as long as I live, I shall live in her. Were I master of an artist's brush, how differently, dear Grandmother, would I glorify you!

But you used to say, "Upon this earthy ball, not a soul that pleases all." If then, a few readers shall find as much pleasure in reading about you as I do in writing, I shall be content.

Němcová, Božena. *Babička* (*The Grandmother*). Trans. Frances Gregor. Vitalis, 2006. 9.

Her *Grandmother*

The loveliest flower in that wreath was our gentle [national] awakener and exceedingly fertile writer, the patriotic Božena Němcová...then at the peak of her literary activity.

Her Grandmother was going from hand to hand and was read with real enthusiasm.

Reminiscences of Václav Pok Poděbradský. Originally published in Záhoř, translated by Iggers, *Women of Prague*, 55.

My Grandmother

I was also raised mostly in German, and only my grandmother, a sincere, old time Czech such as we can still find in Bohemia today, except that no one pays attention to them, admonished me to love our fatherland and told me events from Czech history.

She liked most to tell me about Libuše and Přemysl and always tried to turn me against the German language.

I obeyed her as long as I was little.

Letter from BN to Vrbíková, 22 January 1851. Iggers, *Women of Prague*, 58.

Princess Libuše

The origin of Prague goes back to the 7th century and the Slavic princess Libuše. A legend says that one day Libuše had a vision. She stood on a cliff overlooking the Vltava, pointed to a forested hill across the river, and proclaimed:

> "I see a great city whose glory will touch the stars."

> *"Vidím město veliké, jehož sláva hvězd se dotýkati bude."*

She instructed her people to go and build a castle where a man was building the threshold (in Czech *práh*) of a house. "And because even the great noblemen must bow low before a threshold, you shall give it the name Praha."

Cordini, Lorenzo. "Czech Legends." *My Czech Republic.*

The legend contends that Princess Libuše took the ploughman Přemysl to be her husband; thus began the Přemyslid Dynasty.

The First Great Work of Modern Czech Fiction

It is fitting, then, that the first great work of modern Czech fiction should have been written by a woman, has an ordinary woman for its heroine, and is neither a grand epic nor a great romance but a set of unpretentious "pictures from country life."

Sayers, *Prague: Capital of the Twentieth Century*, 188–89.

In No Land Has Literature Played a Greater Part

in educating and developing national instinct and
ideals. In countries untrammelled by the rigors of a
stiff Austrian censorship of every spoken word, it is
possible to train patriots in schools, auditoriums,
churches. The confiscation of Czech newspapers for
even a remote criticism of the Habsburg government
was a regular thing long before the exigencies of war
made such a proceeding somewhat excusable.

It was then through belles-lettres that the training
for freedom had to come. And the writers of the nation
were ready for they had been prepared for the task
by the spiritual inheritance from their inspired predecessors.
And so it came about that in their effort to express
the soul of the nation they told in every form of literature
of the struggles to maintain lofty aspirations
and spiritual ideals.

Hrbková, Šárka B. Introduction. *Czechoslovak Stories.*

Lineation follows the formatting of the digitalized version.

The Life of Our Nation

She said that with her own soul she agrees with the aims of the nationalists to liberate themselves from the...fetters which have been repressing the life of our nation for ages. She sincerely pressed the hand of each of us students.

She was really ideally beautiful and each of her movements testified to the lofty spirit which resided in that harmonious body.

Reminiscences of Václav Pok Poděbradský about Němcová's stay in Nymburk, a contrast to Kateřina Emlerová-Dlabačová's account of the same time. Originally published in Záhoř, translated by Iggers, *Women of Prague*, 55.

My Good Grandmother

When I was growing up I developed a great liking for German books, and considered Czech literature and the Czech language unrefined.

I had been married for a few years when I first saw Tyl's work; they moved my heart and vividly brought to my mind my good grandmother. She stood before me splendid and beautiful, a picture of sincere, patriotic love.

The memories of my childhood years were revived in my soul.

Letter from BN to Vrbíková, 22 Jan 1851. Iggers, *Women of Prague*, 58.

Němcová is referring to the work of Josef Tyl, a writer and patriot about ten years her senior, who is most famous today for penning *"Kde domov můj?"* ("Where is my home?"), the lyrics of the Czech National Anthem.

Why Grandma, You Have But Four Teeth!

She smiled, smoothed down Barunka's dark brown hair, and said: "My child, I am old; when you grow old, you, too, will look different." But they could not comprehend how their smooth, soft hands could ever become wrinkled like hers.

Němcová, *Babička* (*The Grandmother*). Trans. Gregor, 16.

What the Children Liked Best Was the Large Flowered Chest

On one side of the chest was a small drawer, and what treasures were in that! Family documents and letters, a small linen bag full of silver dollars. Five strings of garnets. A silver coin on which was engraved the picture of Emperor Joseph and Maria Theresa.

When she opened the box—and she always did so whenever the children asked her—she would say, "See, my children, these garnets were given me by your grandfather for my wedding, and this dollar the Emperor Joseph himself gave me. Well, when I die all this will be yours."

Němcová, *Babička* (*The Grandmother*). Trans. Gregor, 16.

What treasures

A Mode of Remembering

If we consider this book we should realize that Czech literature, unlike for instance English literature in the mid 19th century, did not have a novel at that time. What did exist at that time was the short story, but among many of them it had problems with schematic plots, that were often shaped by Czech nationalist ideologies of the time and by didacticism.

Němcová avoided these dangers by using a mode of remembering.

Němcová ingeniously used the language means of an oral narrative. It means the rhythm of spoken sentences and even the vocabulary must have sounded very authentic, not the artificial intellectual language that the Czech intellectuals in Prague tried to invent.

This was authentic.

Higgins, Bernie, and David Vaughan. "Božena Němcová—the Mother of Czech Prose," *Radio Prague*, 2004. Interview with Eva Kalivodová.

Translators, biographers, and fairy tale writers are often faced with challenges pertaining to authenticity. Němcová seems to have found "the entire question of 'authenticity'" to be distasteful. This passage suggests that it was her distaste that, contradictorily, made her work most authentic. Her approach was to use a more flexible "mode of remembering."

Now What Does This Have to Do with *The Castle*, You Ask?

Well, this novel proved to be one of Kafka's favorite books ever since he read it as a child—as an assignment for his Czech class.

The idyllic locale and, especially, the fact that the children
in the story were happy with their parents

affected him strongly, since his own life with his parents
was considerably less than idyllic. This book

was also Milena Jesenská's favorite novel, and she would later write
that her own grandmother was exactly like the one in the novel.

"Božena Němcová—*Babička.*" *Fortune City.*

Kafka's Encounter

A recent rereading of this fragment, with its haunting power and mysterious overtones, reminded me of a still earlier germ for *The Castle*. This was connected with Kafka's encounter with a work by the Czech woman writer Božena Němcová, whose influence upon him has, as far as I know, gone unremarked.

Her principal work, *The Grandmother*, an idyllic novel of masterful simplicity, was used at the Prague German gymnasium as the basis for instruction in the Czech language. That is where Kafka became acquainted with the remarkably appealing, sincere, and upright tale of a village at the foot of the Riesengebirge.

I, too, read it in school a year later, and fell equally in love with it.

Brod, *Franz Kafka: A Biography*, 249–50.

Němcová's influence on Kafka is being remarked upon more and more. In a 1993 article Milan Kundera identifies the parallel settings of *The Grandmother* and *The Castle* and notes that Kafka "filled both the castle and the village with endless official archives and bureaus." Likewise in *Prague Palimpsest*, Alfred Thomas posits in 2010 that, "the bewilderingly disconnected world of *The Castle* is inconceivable without the harmonious nexus between the village and the manor house in *Granny*" (80). And the editors of *The Czech Reader*, also published in 2010, note that, "From this work of 1855, later much admired by Franz Kafka, there is a direct line to the novels of Hašek, Hrabal, and many other contemporary Czech authors" (152).

As Max Brod Has Pointed Out

in his essay on *The Castle*, "Thoughts on *The Castle*," there are more than a few similarities between *Babička* and *The Castle*. Admittedly, the tones of the works are completely different,

> *Babička* being a happy childhood story

> and *The Castle* a disturbing tale of intrigue, despair, and searching,

but nevertheless the similarities, along with some differences, are striking:

> In *Babička*, everybody is happy.   In *The Castle*, nobody is happy.

"Božena Němcová–*Babička*." *Fortune City.*

A Happy Woman!

Granny ends with the phrase, *"Šťastná to žena!"* which translates as "A happy (or fortunate) woman!" Along with the opening couplet of Karel Hynek Mácha's "May," these are among the best-known words in Czech literature.

They could hardly be applied to Božena Němcová herself. Nor could we describe Milena Jesenská as conspicuously *šťastná* in either sense of the word. A very Czech connection is nonetheless there in both cases, because we are in the realm of Czech desires and Czech dreams. By the lights of her time Jesenská was a remarkably independent woman—as was Němcová.

Sayers, *Prague: Capital of the Twentieth Century*, 190.

The Woman Behind the Image

Hello and welcome to Czech books
which this week will be looking at the Czech icon
And—in the words of Milan Kundera—
the mother of Czech prose.

We'd like today to dig a bit deeper
into the reality—

the woman behind the image.

Higgins and Vaughan, "Božena Němcová—the Mother of Czech Prose."

Peter Kussi's translation of Kundera's original quote from his 1993 article in *Cross Currents*, "Three Contexts of Art: From Nation to World," uses the less-gendered term, "founder of Czech prose."

Viktorka Was a Girl as Fresh as a Raspberry

Viktorka is the daughter of a farmer from Zernov. Her parents are dead and buried long ago, but she still has a brother and sister living. Fifteen years ago Viktorka was a girl as fresh as a raspberry; search high and low and you wouldn't find the fellow to her. Lissom as a doe, diligent as a bee, nobody could have wished for a finer wife. A girl like that, especially when she had a share in a farm coming to her, doesn't stay long on the shelf, that's pretty evident.

Her fame had gone round all the neighborhood, and the suitors came thick to the door. Many a one of them would have pleased her father and mother well enough, more than one was a rich farmer, and the daughter would have come into her fortune, as they say, but she didn't want to pay any attention to such considerations.

The only one who got into her favor was the one who danced best, and even he only as long as the music lasted.

(In *Babička*, everybody is happy.)

Němcová, *Babička* (*The Grandmother*). Trans. by Gregor, 16.

My addition of the parenthetical line from the *Fortune City* website.

So This Is Viktorka. Could You Say a Little More About Her Story?

Well, Viktorka is in fact counterpointed to the Grandmother in this narrative.

Definitely these two are the two central characters.

But there are many more characters on the scene of the narrative, on the scene of one village, where they just live, work, meet, talk, and experience things together. And most of them enjoy the company of Babička, the Grandmother, who is the source of active and helpful goodness and generosity and common sense, guiding other people in life. This is a very complex world of its own, pulsing with life through the four seasons of the year. It may seem to be an idyll, but *Babička* is not an idyll, because there is this one character of Viktorka, whose fate is very dark, and it's a very dark counterpoint to the Grandmother's.

(In *Babička*, everybody is happy.)

Higgins and Vaughan, "Božena Němcová—the Mother of Czech Prose."

Viktorka, Whose Fate Is Very Dark

Viktorka is a young woman, whose passionate love for a mysteriously romantic figure of a lover becomes a way to self-destruction.

And Viktorka, after probably being betrayed by her lover, returns to the village, and she returns mad and mute.

She cannot talk any more.

She remains in the woods and she is only full of grief.

There are hardly any human needs left in her, and she cannot be helped by Babička.

That's probably the only character which cannot be helped by Babička.

(In *Babička*, everybody is happy.)

Higgins and Vaughan, "Božena Němcová—the Mother of Czech Prose."

Poor Viktorka

a half-mad peasant girl roaming through the forests.

Critics and film producers have long felt that Božena Němcová hid

many of her own passions in   Viktorka, the girl seduced

by a soldier and left with a child
whom she drowns.

Demetz, *Prague in Black and Gold*, 312.

A Lake

My soul is often as a lake, where a slight wind stirs up waves that cannot be calmed.

One thought chases the other as little clouds in a thunder storm, each more somber than the next, until the whole sky is covered

with heavy clouds...

Letter from BN to unknown addressee (probably Jurenka), 1854. Iggers, *Women of Prague*, 64.

Kafka's Special Ghostly Note

It seems to me that Kafka's equivocal melody in *The Castle* is sounded here clearly enough. It occurs often in the subsequent pages of the Czech novel. This is Kafka's special ghostly note, but it is not altogether alien to Němcová's straightforward realism. The suggestion was there, and Kafka found it in his youthful reading. He turned it to his own purposes, raised it from an incidental detail to a mighty principle.

Brod, *Franz Kafka: A Biography*, 249–50.

Relatedly, Kundera argues for the importance of reading both Kafka and Němcová in their Central European context. He claims that "Germanistics and Slavistics," in attempting to emphasize either the German or Czech contexts of these authors, have lost the significance of their interconnectivity.

Viktorka's Sorrowful and Broken Melody

Grandmother looks up into the branches, hears gentle sighs, low twittering, and peeping. "They are dreaming of something," she says and goes further. What has delayed her by the garden?

Does she hear the pleasant warbling of two nightingales in the garden shrubbery, or Viktorka's sorrowful and broken melody that resounds from the dam? Or has she turned her eyes to the hill where multitudes of fire-flies are shining like so many twinkling stars?

Němcová, *Babička* (*The Grandmother*). Trans. Gregor, 154–55.

Ukolébavka Z Viktorka

Spi, dětátko, spi
zamhuř očka svý,
Pánbůh bude s tebou spáti,
andělíčky kolébati—
spi, dětátko, spi.

Viktorka's Lullaby

Sleep, my baby, sleep
Close your eyelids, sweet,
God himself will slumber with you,
And his angels rock and guard you—
Sleep, my baby, sleep.

Němcová, *Babička* (*The Grandmother*). Trans. Gregor, 98.

Singing That Lullaby

Since that time she is at the bank every evening
singing that lullaby.

In the morning I told my master, and he guessed at once
what she most probably threw into the water—and it was true.

When we saw her again, her form was changed.

Her mother and the others shuddered; but what could be done?
The unknowing cannot sin!

Němcová, *Babička* (*The Grandmother*). Trans. Gregor, 98.

how Dickens, for example, would have handled the same scene. In Němcová's novel, Viktorka's deed is recognized as desperately sad, but the writing is completely unmelodramatic and, more importantly, uncensorious. Gregorová's translation follows Němcová meticulously: the tragedy is related in simple but powerful language and is thereby all the more effective.

Partridge, James. "Review of *The Grandmother.*" *Central Europe Review.* Vol. 1, No. 7, August 1999. Partridge clarifies that the translation was "by Františka Gregorová (writing under the name Frances Gregor) and originally published in Chicago in 1892." Partridge likewise notes that: "some of the darker or more ambiguous aspects of the novel are played down or even overlooked. Němcová's unhappiness and suffering in the 1850s left its mark on *Babička*, as did her concerns with the Czech national identity."

Poor Viktorka

Viktorka lives in a cave, wanders through the woods, gathers berries, and snatches pieces of bread left for her on the windowsills by peasants

—until she is killed in the woods by lightning.

(In *Babička*, everybody is happy.)

Demetz, *Prague in Black and Gold,* 313.

The Dark Femininity of Viktorka

brings tragic
      love protest seduction
unwanted   (pregnancy)   murder
                  madness

a figure who   exclusion, solitude

      the unspeakable

Šmejkalová, "Božena Němcová," *Biographical Dictionary of Women's Movements*, 369.

The Real Viktorka

was an alcoholic mother of two, who miserably died on the road not long after the novel was published.

Demetz, *Prague in Black and Gold*, 313.

Viktorka's Lullaby Was Heard No More

by the dam; the cave was empty;
the fir above it cut down;

still she was by no means forgotten.

Němcová, *Babička* (*The Grandmother*). Trans. Gregor, 310.

The Forest Women Dance by the Light of the Moon

Below the hill over the meadow are hovering clouds like waves of gossamer. The people say they are not clouds, and perhaps she, too, believes that in those transparent silver gray veils are enrobed the forest women, and is now watching their wild dance by the light of the moon.

Grandmother remains standing in a deep reverie.

Němcová, *Babička* (*The Grandmother*). Trans. Gregor, 155.

Grandmother Was Failing

People did not know how Grandmother was failing; she alone felt it. She would often say to Adélka, pointing to an old apple tree that year by year grew dryer and put on its green foliage more sparingly: "We are alike; we shall probably go to sleep together."

One spring, when all the other trees were clad in their green livery, the old apple tree stood there alone, without a single leaf.

Her memory began to fail. She often called Barunka instead of Adélka, and when the latter reminded her that Barunka was not at home, recollecting herself she would say, sighing deeply:

"No, no, she is not at home.
Is she happy?"

Němcová, *Babička* (*The Grandmother*). Trans. Gregor, 329–30.

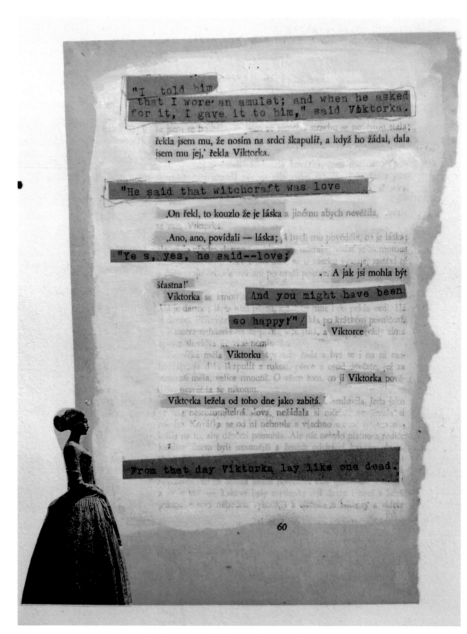

"I told him that I wore an amulet; and when he asked for it, I gave it to him," said Viktorka.

řekla jsem mu, že nosím na srdci škapulíř, a když ho žádal, dala isem mu jej,' řekla Viktorka.

"He said that witchcraft was love

,On řekl, to kouzlo že je láska a jinému abych nevěřila,

,Ano, ano, povídali — láska;

"Ye s, yes, he said--love;

. A jak jsi mohla být šťastna!'

Viktorka

And you might have been so happy!"

Viktorce

Viktorku

Viktorka

Viktorka ležela od toho dne jako zabitá.

From that day Viktorka lay like one dead.

60

And you might have been so happy!

Sleep, my baby, sleep

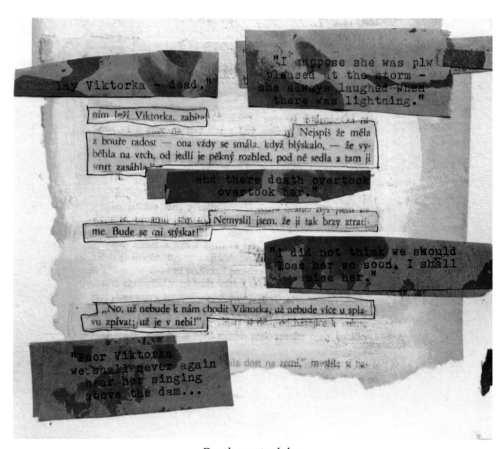

"I suppose she was plw pleased at the storm — she always laughed when there was lightning."

lay Viktorka — dead."

ním leží Viktorka, zabita

z bouře radost — ona vždy se smála, když blýskalo, — že vyběhla na vrch, od jedlí je pěkný rozhled, pod ně sedla a tam ji smrt zasáhla

yl Nejspíš že měla

and there death overtook overtook her."

Nemyslil jsem, že ji tak brzy ztratíme. Bude se mi stýskat!"

"I did not think we should lose her so soon. I shall miss her."

„No, už nebude k nám chodit Viktorka, už nebude více u splavu zpívat; už je v nebi!"

"Poor Viktorka we shall never again hear her singing above the dam...

Death overtook her

She lives on

I see a great city whose glory will touch the stars

Is she happy?

5. The Beautiful Star of Love

Decline

When *The Grandmother* appeared in 1855, the decline in Němcová's life had already set in: her search for an ideal love...was almost over. She had been abandoned by many of her friends, her son Hynek was dead, her son Karel had not written from Germany for almost a year, her youngest son, Jarous, had given up his art studies in Munich for financial reasons, and her only daughter, Dora, was constantly sick. Her husband's career had gone from bad to worse, and he was continually being banished to work in distant, isolated places.

Iggers, *Women of Prague*, 50.

My Body Sinks

What should I write to you?
One blow follows the other, my body sinks,
I don't know how long I'll be able to stand it.
Since my good Hynek's death I have been sick constantly,
a worm against which there is no medicine eats away at my organism.
Besides there is my terrible worry about my family's well-being.

Letter from BN to Alois Vojtěch Šembera, 26 August 1856. Iggers, *Women of Prague*, 73.

Šembera was a fellow writer and patriot, very active in the Czech revival.

Women's Work

I cannot make a living with literature.

But things are even worse with women's work—

So what am I to do?

I was supposed to go as a companion to a lady in the madhouse—I was attracted by the good pay—She suddenly began to rage so much, that only strong maids could be with her.

I have debts...I have sold everything of any value...we are often hungry...

I have buried many of my hopes and beautiful ideals.

Letter from BN to Šembera, 26 August 1856. Iggers, *Women of Prague*, 73.

If I Could Pull Myself Together and Write

I am wondering, if you ever send anything to Prague, if it would be possible for you to send us a few potatoes...

don't be angry, but I have nothing for the winter...

I don't know what to do for a living.

Even if in all this sorrow I could pull myself together and write, there would be no buyers.

Letter from BN to Josef Hostivít Hušek. 5 Nov 1853. Iggers, *Women of Prague*, 64.

Iggers calls Hušek a friend of Němcová's and "a farm manager in Jindice" (63). This letter is written just two weeks after the death of her son Hynek. In it Němcová says that even Hynek's funeral was considered a patriotic demonstration: "One suffers from the sin of being a Czech, standing by one's nationality and loving one's brothers in language more than distant neighbors. Why this distrust of Slavs who have sufficiently proven their honesty and loyal sentiments?" (64).

Day After Day She Wrote

long into the night, although she was not well.

She shared her last bite with me and with the children, the poor things who also rarely ate their fill.

Often we ate...prunes and...bread for two kreuzers a day.

Reminiscences of Marie Langhammerová, Božena Němcová's former maid. Originally published in Záhoř, translated by Iggers, *Women of Prague*, 68.

A Terribly Poor Thing

You know that somebody who supports herself by literature is a terribly poor thing.

I won't be offended if you don't take anything...but if you keep the story, I beg you to send me at least part of the honorarium if possible.

Letter from BN to Helcelet, 18–19 June 1856, after their affair had ended. Iggers, *Women of Prague*, 69.

Jan Neruda

Our glances wandered over the poor worn furniture, and kept returning to the faded, bluish table cloth; to this day I see those holes in it, mended with large white stitches. We had perhaps experienced even greater poverty, but that we should have seen it with a celebrated person as the result of a life full of work...

Němcová came in a cotton shirt, with a silken but very old black collar. She sat down on the worn and bumpy sofa...she was so thin and her deep eyes burned in a fever!

We went silently down the stairs.

We too were determined to "devote ourselves to literature."

Reminiscences of Jan Neruda, who visited BN with the poet Vitězslav Hálek in Prague. Originally published in Záhoř, translated by Iggers, *Women of Prague*, 68.

Jan Neruda (1834–1891) is buried across from Němcová in Prague's National Cemetery in Vyšehrad. The author of *Povídky malostranské* (*Tales of the Lesser Quarter*), published in 1877, Neruda is known for his realistic portrayals of urban Czech life and interest in social issues. He also was in love with Němcová's friend and rival, Karolina Světlá. Because she was already married, their relationship was primarily epistolary.

We too were determined to "devote ourselves to literature."

I Was Hemorrhaging

You probably wonder why this Božena is not publishing The Grandmother.

On the way I already felt I was hemorrhaging...

When I was alone in my room, I took out my own sheet and waxed cloth, spread them on the sofa and prepared a clean bandage. In the morning I asked the old nursemaid if she knew of anyone who could launder my blood stained underwear while I waited.

She brought me a glass of milk and two crescent rolls.

Letter from BN to Vojtěch Náprstek, 21 November 1861. Iggers, *Women of Prague*, 83.

God Knows

I am becoming
weaker every day.
I can't even think

of going to the country, being all ragged.
The black dress is worn and the silk one
would go badly with the torn shoes.
My shirts are also tearing.

God knows how things will be
with my health.

Letter from BN to her husband, 31 July 1857. Iggers, *Women of Prague*, 81.

Although this letter and a few others were written several years before Němcová's death, Iggers notes this year as the beginning of her decline. Likewise, according to Jiřina Šmejkalová: "The year 1857 was marked by Němcová's first creative writing crisis and increasing financial desperation" (368).

But I Am No Longer

     young

   and was chosen not to love

but to suffer.

Letter from BN to unknown addressee, undated. Iggers, *Women of Prague*, 61.

Sometimes the Longing

to lie down on your chest
and cry

comes to me. I know   my only refuge is
            there.

You used to say   I don't   value you,

and that quite different ideals   are in my   soul...I don't
deny that I once had   an ideal of how marriage

and a husband should be—Well,

        I was young, inexperienced.

Letter from BN to her husband, 31 July 1857. Iggers, *Women of Prague,* 81.

My Soul Burned

with desire

for education, for something

       higher,

and with disgust   for vulgarity

this was my fortune, but also the cause of
our rift, my unhappiness.

Letter from BN to her husband, 31 July 1857. Iggers, *Women of Prague*, 81.

It Is a Strange Life Between Us

—sometimes I almost feel sorry for him,

         and I reproach myself for being so hard on him—

Letter from BN to Helcelet, 18–19 June 1856. Iggers, *Women of Prague*, 81.

You Had My Body, My Actions, My Honesty

     but my desires

went further—I myself did not understand
where...

     I was longing
     I wanted

to fill the

                empty space

     in my soul

with something,
but I had   no idea
what it could be.

First I thought   it could be
love   for a man...
now I know that this was not
     true. I

embraced the national idea
with all my heart, but even that

     did not

Letter from BN to her husband, 31 July 1857. Trans. Šmejkalová, "Božena Němcová,"
Biographical Dictionary of Women's Movements, 369.

I Am Surprised We Are Still in This World

That we have neither died of suffering nor ended it all ourselves.

It is terrible how fate plays with us, and just now when one is at the end of one's life, so to speak.

We are both unhappy creatures and I would be unhappier if I didn't have you; believe me, you are the only soul that gives me strength in this misery.

Who knows where I would be without you
without you the world is...

Letter to BN from her husband, 14 December 1856. Iggers, *Women of Prague*, 76.

Empty

You are not legally divorced and therefore cannot live away from your husband without his permission. If you intend to be divorced from me legally, do it in the proper place...you spoke

empty words, as usual.

The children have known their loving mother for a long time. I can imagine that you won't like the way I am speaking to you. I always speak and act openly.

Your still legal husband, Němec

Summary by Josef Lelek of letter from Josef Němec to BN, 21 November 1861. Translated by Iggers, *Women of Prague*, 84.

In 1860 the strained couple decided to divorce, if not quite legally, then by mutual agreement. This letter was written just a few months before Němcová's death.

Josef Němec

He was a born—and also well-trained—storyteller, who as the occasion demanded was able to make use of illustrative epithets, folk sayings, comparisons, well-chosen words, exclamations, abbreviations, and allusions.

Quote by Miloslav Novotný. Transcribed from a display at the Muzeum Boženy Němcové.

Mr. Vojtěch!

When I left Prague, I was determined not to return to my husband. In the morning he began screaming and calling me names...and didn't care if a maid was there. When I tried to protect Dora from his beating, he hit me—and at that time I was already sick.

When somebody...asked why I was not writing anything, he said:
    "She will never write anything again, she is dumb.
    She belongs in the mad house."

When he saw me writing, he extinguished my lamp, and said that it was not my petroleum.

One afternoon he came home, and I was just organizing the fairy tales into a volume. He grabbed it, threw it on the floor and began tearing it up.

At that point I became angry and tore it out of his hand, and when he did not want to let me go,

I bit his hand until he began to bleed.

Letter from BN to Vojtěch Náprstek, 11 November 1861. Iggers, *Women of Prague*, 82.

Josef Němec

My custom is always to act and speak clearly, without ulterior motives.

Letter from Josef Němec to BN, 21 Sept. 1861. Transcribed from a display at the Muzeum Boženy Němcové.

So I Suffered

What all I have been through!
And how Dad has always behaved towards me these last 23 years we've
been together!
I would not have stayed with him one year if it had not been for you.
So I suffered for you what few women have suffered.

In order not to be dependent on Dad for everything,
I became a writer—

Letter from BN to her son Karel, 5 February 1860. Iggers, *Women of Prague*, 82.

The Beautiful Star of Love

Look, Adéla, marriage can be heaven where there is love and mutual respect, but it becomes hell   when it descends to meanness.

When I felt the most unhappy,   the beautiful star of love arose for me—

as if by a miracle, poetry awakened me to life in my unhappiness!

It sweetens my life, and I have consecrated myself to it for all eternity! It taught me to love people, it prevented me from drowning in vulgarity, it ennobled me.

It also provided peace in my marriage.

Once the feeling of true love has fallen into one's heart, one keeps it until death; like a bright drop of amber which can neither dry up nor sink into the ground.

Such love shines in one's breast!

Letter from BN to her sister Adéla, 21 November 1856. Iggers, *Women of Prague*, 73–74.

The Little Stars of Gold, Part Three

All at once, she saw little stars falling in her pathway. She wanted to see what they looked like. They were yellow, bright and shining. She began to gather them up in her hands, tossing them up and down. "Oh, if I only had an apron." Why there was an apron! Then she collected the little yellow stars in her apron, and growing very tired, fell asleep.

Němcová, "Little Stars of Gold."

A Troubled Sleep

On January 20, 1861 she received her author's copy of the first edition of *Babička*.

She burst into tears over it, because it was printed with so many mistakes and on the cheapest paper.

Although she felt no pain, she was weakened further by this and fell into a troubled sleep.

"Božena Němcová," *Radio Prague's Virtual Cemetery.*

It's not clear why she was receiving a copy of *Babička's* first edition in 1861, six years after its publication. More likely is that she received a copy of the newest edition. This takes place one year before her death.

I Don't Sleep

I don't sleep, all night
the most terrible thoughts

                              persecute me

it's a wonder
that I am   not   going   crazy

          I have a fever
          every
          day.

Letter from BN to her husband, 31 July 1857. Iggers, *Women of Prague*, 81.

Asleep and Sleep

Sometimes   when I go to bed in the evening   I only wish

        I would fall

                                    asleep and sleep

                a long, long...

Letter from BN to Bendl, 21 February 1857. Iggers, *Women of Prague*, 78.

She Never Woke

Her husband then brought a priest to give her the Last Sacrament,
but she never woke again.

"Božena Němcová," *Radio Prague's Virtual Cemetery.*

Dreams

Němcová didn't live to see the man of her dreams.

"Božena Němcová," *Radio Prague's Virtual Cemetery.*

In a Dream

I tried to go to the kitchen...there lay a large snake on the doorstep, with his mouth open.

I screamed and woke up. It was bright daylight.

Letter from BN to Bendl, 21 February 1857. Iggers, *Women of Prague*, 78.

The Little Stars of Gold, Part Four

Awaking very early in the morning, to her surprise, there was one of the little stars making itself into a pancake for her breakfast! She ate all she

could and still had some left.

After wandering a great distance, she reached her aunt's hut in the evening. After kissing her aunt, she said, "Oh, auntie, see what I have in my apron." Instead of the little stars which she expected to see, a stream of gold pieces

poured out of her apron and rolled all over the room.
Imagine the surprise and joy of the poor old woman. Now she could not only support Božena, but could do much good for others all the rest of

her life.

Němcová, "Little Stars of Gold."

Elements of the Fairy Tale

Němcová's own life contained elements of the fairy tale:
her parentage was possibly noble, though she was raised among the household servant class;
she was forced to marry a man she did not love;
unwise decisions brought her personal hardship later in life as well as financial troubles;
and she came to an untimely end.

"Božena Němcová," *Encyclopedia of World Biography.*

Death Came to Her

softly—she slipped away at six
in the morning on January 21, 1862.

In a few days she would have been forty-two

or forty-three

or even forty-five years old.

"Božena Němcová," *Radio Prague's Virtual Cemetery.*

Because Němcová's birth records have been called into question, it is no longer certain
that she was born in 1820; thus, it is unclear how old she was at the time of her death.

The News of Her Death

was carried
　　　　by all the Czech
and German newspapers in Prague

a thousand people　　　　her funeral procession
　　　　prayers coffin church Vyšehrad
　　　　carried out
into the freezing dusk
the cemetery
the flickering

candlelight.

"Božena Němcová," *Radio Prague's Virtual Cemetery.*

My Husband Began Screaming and Calling Me Names

"You good for nothing. You will croak somewhere behind a fence, nobody will even spit at you, you should be selling matches."

Letter from BN to Náprstek, 11 November 1861, just months before her death. Iggers, *Women of Prague*, 82-83.

In this letter Němcová narrates an ugly scene with her husband, which culminated in the above comment by her husband. "And so it went on every day," she writes.

The Death of Božena Němcová

The windows all are open—There is death

Her soul departed like a flare of light
Only candles watch the passing of her breath
The heart stops at last—And silent yet weeping
The women leave the body clean and sleeping
Sleep Yellow and hollow is the dead alas
A star in decline—Aurora trims her head
She would have liked to sow some seeds of wrath.

Peaslee, "Božena Němcová Remembered."

This is from a series of poems by František Halas, provided in translation on Peaslee's website. Halas was a twentieth-century poet whose series of poems, *Our Lady Božena Němcová*, was published in 1942. A couple years earlier, Jaroslav Seifert, who would go on to become the first Czechoslovak to win the Nobel Prize in literature in 1984, published an as-yet untranslated collection of poems called *Božena Němcová's Fan* (1940). Both were written during the Nazi occupation of Czechoslovakia and reflect the renewed struggle for national identity.

Poetry

Poetry is, in times of joy but also in times of trial and peril, the true expression of the whole nation whose only mouthpiece remains the poet.

Peaslee, "Božena Němcová Remembered."

Men

Němcová has often reminded men of the traditional idea of the Virgin Mary.

Iggers, *Women of Prague*, 49.

Women

While women have focused on the unhappily married, misunderstood wife, the woman deserted by her lovers, the mother who—like the Virgin Mary—lost her beloved son.

Iggers, *Women of Prague*, 49.

However, while she was alive, the "women of Prague" (to borrow Iggers' title) were scandalized by Němcová's behaviors. After her death, the focus of her legacy shifted to her writing and her dedication to the national cause. As time has passed, these views have continued to grow and change, and her personal life has become more central again. Moving forward, as Jiřina Šmejkalová writes: "We need to examine the capacity of her writings to reveal the limits of naming women's desire and experiences within the dominant symbolic and social order" (369).

I Heard

that Mrs. Němcová suffered. They say

 she died of starvation.

It's a shame about her...

  May God give her eternal glory!

Reminiscences of Mrs. Podestátová. Originally published in Záhoř, translated by Iggers, *Women of Prague*, 55.

I Still See Her

entering our living room...she was like a radiant light falling into my soul.

Then thirty years old, she looked like nineteen—so marvelous was her complexion, so radiant her eyes, so slender, nimble was her figure. She wore a white hat, a sand colored dress, tight fitting, with a fringed skirt, and over it a black velvet jacket down to her hips. All in extremely good taste and elegant. Her wonderful black hair was combed smoothly along her temples and twisted behind in a simple Grecian knot.

Thus lives her likeness in my memory.

Reminiscences of Žofie Podlipská. Originally published in Záhoř, translated by Iggers, *Women of Prague*, 56.

Although Podlipská's relationship with Němcová cooled after those intense years in the early 1850s, she maintained affection for Němcová.

It Is Impossible To Forget Her

Božena's life could have been quite different, but this was not possible in view of her trusting, unrealistic, poetic nature.

Worries, poverty, difficulties killed her, aggravated her sickness which cut her life short. How much love and gentleness there was in her, how much beauty, what fascinating ideas.

No, it is impossible to forget her.

Reminiscences of Anna Cardová-Lamblová, sister of Vilém Dušan Lambl. Originally published in Záhoř, translated by Iggers, *Women of Prague*, 66.

She Wanted

to live only by the pen
and perhaps even paid for it with her life.

Němcová was absolutely not the victim
      of hunger and poverty

some people make her out to be   she consciously sacrificed herself
to her most intimate, sacred conviction

            the wings of her creativity.

Reminiscences of Karolina Světlá. Originally published in Záhoř, translated by Iggers *Women of Prague*, 57.

Světlá walks a fine line in her comments about Němcová, but her main goal seems to be the preservation of Němcová's legacy for the nationalist cause.

On the Occasion of the Unveiling of a Statue of Božena Němcová

To mark this memorable place forever:

where the precious spirit of a Czech woman first spread its wings to begin
its blessed flight,
> *where her soul,*
> *where fate—*

her soul   changed every drop of blood   into roses,
eternally blossoming   created by her

> *for pleasure,*
> *past and present.*

Telegram sent by the writer Karolina Světlá, marking the unveiling of a statue of Němcová in August 1888, twenty-five years after her death. Iggers, *Women of Prague*, 86.

Iggers notes the contrast between Světlá's comments here and the ones she made when Němcová was alive.

The Bitter Life of Božena Němcová

Many generations of admiring poets, patriotic critics,
and, at times, official propagandists have long transformed

the bitter life of Božena Němcová,
the first Czech woman writer of importance,

into a cherished national myth.

Demetz, *Prague in Black and Gold*, 308.

A Prematurely Old and Bitter Woman

Němcová's portraits dramatically change from those of a young beauty to a prematurely old and bitter woman.

Iggers, *Women of Prague*, 50.

Her Absolute Refusal To Be Cynical or Bitter

Despite the inevitable sorrows

the fact that all the romance and joy

    was crushed.

Hrbková, Introduction to "Divá Bára," *Czechoslovak Stories*, 148.

Not a Trace of Bitterness Appears

Not a trace of bitterness appears in the entire novel, though it was written when Němcová was experiencing nothing but hardship and sorrow in a most unhappy married life, and after death had removed her chief joy—her eldest son, Hynek.

Hrbková, Introduction to "Divá Bára," *Czechoslovak Stories*, 148.

There Was Not a Drop of Bitterness

As outgoing and lively as Němcová used to be in the company of friends,
she was sad
 when I sometimes found her at home alone.

Then her heart overflowed   with her sorrows.

   There was not a drop of bitterness in her heart.

She did not blame anybody.

Reminiscences of Žofie Podlipská. Originally published in Záhoř, translated by Iggers, *Women of Prague*, 56.

A Drop of Bitterness

Life is very bitter to me.

Letter from BN to Bendl, 21 February 1857. Iggers, *Women of Prague*, 78.

A Drop of Longing

The longing remains

        in my soul as a drop

which neither dries up nor flows away, but eternally
sparkles like a diamond;

  longing

            infinite.

Letter from BN to her husband, 13 Jun 1857. Iggers, *Women of Prague*, 80.

A Drop of Desire

This

        desire

has settled in my soul—

    a little

drop

    which can never dry out.

Letter from BN to her husband, 13 June 1857. Šmejkalová, "Božena Němcová," *Biographical Dictionary of Women's Movements*, 369.

This is the same passage as the previous letter, but this translation by Šmejkalová takes a slightly different tone than Iggers'.

Desire

The irresistible desire impels me here and there;
I would like to bathe my brow in the fires of the sun's rays at one turn,
immerse it into the depths of the sea at another,
and on the pinions of the winds I would like to orbit the world!
With ardent love I embrace the world;

I give love to people—and they—with a pin they lacerate my heart!

My veneration of love they call a sin; for my love of freedom—they crucify me—
when I speak the truth, it is evil, and if I tell a lie, they rail at me!

How can I bear it?

My shoulders are not titanic!·

I am a weak woman—I am sick, I am a sinner!

Němcová, "Čtyry doby," 354.

This piece and the erasures that follow come from the fourth and final section of the story. Riedlbauchová notes that, "The woman climbing a mountain in the fourth chapter seems to be dying—she doesn't know where to go and has to decide for herself. She seeks harmony, but, at the same time, considers suicide" (62).

The Irresistible Desire

impels me here and I would like to bathe my brow
I would like to orbit the world
with ardent love I give love
I speak the truth

How can I?

I am a woman I am I am

The irresistible desire   impels me and I am a woman

The irresistible desire impels me

The irresistible desire—

The Irresistible Desire

                        I would like
I would like
              love I give love
I speak

       I am   I am I am

           desire   I am

              desire   me

                                      irresistible—

I am a woman, I am, I am

Death came to her

Grave

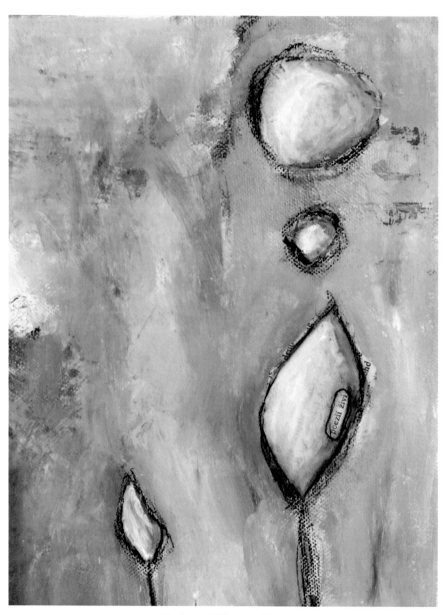

The beautiful star of love

POSTCARDS TO BOŽENA

Writing letters is actually an intercourse with ghosts, and by no means just the ghost of the addressee but also with one's own ghost, which secretly evolves inside the letter one is writing.

—Franz Kafka, *Letters to Milena*

Dear Božena,

My happiness was a heap of half-broken things called togetherness.

k.

Dear B.,

And what of your happiness, your bitterness?

It was 2012: *Rok Boženy Němcové*, the Year of Božena Němcová. One hundred fifty years of death. More than three times longer than your life. I was trying to know you, but I didn't even speak your language.

k.

Dear B.,

The first week of Czech language class was how are you, where are you from, what do you do. *Jak se máte? Odkud jste? Co děláte?* The first week was I'm fine, I'm from America, I'm a professor. *Mám se dobře. Jsem z Ameriky. Jsem profesorka.* I must have said *jsem profesorka* a hundred times.

On a smoke break the second week my teacher Luděk told me that in Czech, the word "professor" is rarely used and reflects the highest level of prestige. I might as well have been telling my class I was the President. In the U.S., I was a newly tenured professor. In Prague I didn't know who I was.

k.

Dear B.,

Who was I? My Slovak relatives wanted to know. How was I related to them? After three weeks of Czech class I took a train to Slovakia, to my great-grandparents' village of Okoličné surrounded by the High Tatra Mountains, where I met second and third cousins; only Marta, my mom's age, spoke English.

I strung together a few words of explanation in a language close enough to theirs: "*Můj dědeček je synem Zuzka Salisová.*" My grandfather is the son of Susan Salish, to whom they were all related.

Why was I studying Czech? They wanted to know. The implication was that I should be studying Slovak. "*Studuji Božena Němcová,*" I told them with my limited vocabulary. They nodded and smiled in approval.

k.

Dear B.,

Why was I studying Czech? The implication for Czechs was that I shouldn't be studying it at all: "There are only 10 million Czech speakers in the world. It is the hardest language to learn. As hard as Chinese!"

But everyone at the language school had a reason: Seventy-year-old Hoshi-san from Japan wanted to give a wedding speech to his son's Czech bride in her language. Valerie from France was in a university exchange program. Rachel from Missouri thought it would be a fun way to fulfill her college language requirement. Madison and Alyssa from Alabama were planning to be missionaries in Olomouc. Jenelle from Canada was writing her dissertation on Czech artists. Vladimir from Russia was doing business in Prague. Lauren from Colorado was studying medieval Bohemian bones. I wanted to read your letters, to know you better. I wanted a month away from my marriage.

k.

Dear B.,

And I wanted a Czech typewriter. If only I could type ž, ě, and á! But every day in Prague required multiple acts of bravery. I was often lost, on the wrong tram, or headed in the wrong direction. And alone. I am very brave, or at least somewhat brave, when I am with other people. Even an antique store requires bravery. But I really wanted a Czech typewriter, and I love antique stores, which are like free museums where you can touch everything. So I made myself brave and went in.

k.

Dear B.,

Rainer Maria Rilke was born in Prague in 1875, thirteen years after your death. In the fifth letter to the young poet, he says: *What you really need is simply this—aloneness, great inner solitude. To go within and not meet anyone.*

But I was tired of being alone. And there are no Czech typewriters within me.

k.

Dear B.,

The antique shop was full of clocks, the pendulums swinging madly, as if time, in this store that tried to capture time, go back in time, as if time, the ticking seconds of one clock echoed by the next, the seconds, the minutes, the overlapping ticks and clicks, as if time itself was accelerated, hurried, and everything was racing to the end and I was going to be old or dead or both in an hour, tops.

k.

Dear B.,

But I was already old. When Valerie from France, my conversation partner in Czech class, found out my age, her eyes got wide as she realized: "*Jhou could be my mother!*"

Maternally yours,
k.

Dear B.,

Every day I took the twenty-two tram from my rented flat in Vinohrady to my Czech language class in Albertov. One day as I rode home, a plaque on a building caught my eye. I got off at the next stop to investigate. The sign said: *Dům Zrození "Babička" Boženy Němcové.* The house where your *Grandmother* was born.

k.

Tram from Vinohrady

Dear B.,

There was graffiti on the side of the house, a three-story stucco walkup, where you wrote *The Grandmother*. I tried to imagine that it was one hundred and fifty years ago and you were walking out the door, but it didn't work. Prague looks old, but it is very young.

k.

Prague is young

Dear B.,

At the house where *The Grandmother* was born, something else happened many years later, many years ago. There was a sign under your sign. I had to *Google Translate* it:

Here Was Shot by Nazis
On 5 May 1945
Marie Musilová
71 Years
Honor Her Memory

I searched online for Marie Musilová so I could honor her memory, but could only find living versions on social media. As if, despite the Nazi bullets, she were alive now, young, and on Facebook.

k.

Honor her memory

Dear B.,

I prefer the literal translation of *71 Letá*: 71 Summers.

You had only forty-two summers when you died. How was it possible to die at that age? How was it possible to die? In 2012, I had forty-one summers.

Two months earlier, in the spring of her eighty-ninth summer, my Granny looked pensive and my mom said to her, "What are you thinking about, Mom?" And she said, "I'm thinking about dying." A week later she was dead.

k.

Dear B.,

In *The Grandmother*, when the children leave for the first day of school, they tell the Grandmother they will miss her, and she foretells her own death:

I shall miss you too, my children, but it must be so. While the tree is sound, it bears fruit; when it dies they cut it down and cast it into the fire, and the ashes fertilize the soil out of which new trees grow. Thus your Grandmother will finish her tasks, and you will bear her away to her eternal rest.

k.

Dear B.,

After the Grandmother's speech, *from the dam came the sad sound of Viktorka's lullaby.*

Viktorka drowned her baby after the soldier abandoned her, and she lives alone in the woods and sings the baby lullabies each night. *Spi dětátko spi.* Sleep, baby, sleep.

k.

Dear B.,

Viktorka's infatuation with the soldier is half Devil's curse, half bewitchery. The villagers help her fight the attraction with magic: prayers, amulets, guardian angels, and herbal potions. She even tries to protect herself by getting engaged to someone else. But protect herself from what?

Perhaps the only way to tell the story of a girl like Viktorka who lies with a stranger in a field is to say that a voice called her and she was filled with a sudden desire to find a four-leaf clover.

k.

Dear B.,

Whereas in another of your stories, Bewitched Bára is not bewitched at all. The superstitious townspeople think she is a victim of the Noon Witch, that she is a changeling. But she is in fact quite healthy. And in love.

I like both translations of Divá Bára: Bewitched Bára and Wild Bára. Bewitched is how the world has to explain a girl who is wild.

k.

Dear B.,

In your stories love was the proper foundation of marriage—itself a radical idea in the early nineteenth century. You critiqued conventions that kept apart those who loved one another: in "Divá Bára," Elška had to hide her love for her Prague doctor; in *Babička*, the Countess loved her art teacher instead of the Count; Kristla loved Jakub Míla, who was conscripted when a jealous suitor saw that Kristla favored him.

But you also wrote about marriage as a blood sacrifice, as a punishment, as bondage, as death.

k.

Dear B.,

On the first Monday in July 2012 I woke early, jet-lagged, for my first Czech class. I opened my laptop and groggily reviewed the directions to the *škola* before clicking a link to the *Prague Post*. On my screen was a picture of Pearl Jam, whom I'd seen in concert a dozen times in the U.S., but hadn't seen since 2006. They were playing in Prague that night.

Twelve hours later I bought an extra ticket from a guy who'd driven five hours from Poland. His friend wasn't able to come. I sat beside him at the concert, and though we did not speak, though I was ten? fifteen? years older, in my head I said to him: *Touch me. Give me an excuse to leave.*

k.

Dear B.,

I was starting to understand that it was time for my marriage to end—that I might even be ready for it—but I had no idea what to do, how to begin to end it. A "mistake" like that, an accidental fling, would remove some of my agency, would start the process by default. Like knocking over a candle that burns down a house you don't want to live in anymore.

k.

Dear B.,

Sometimes we hide behind language and metaphor. But Czech is often very literal, as in the names of months. It was 2012 and the language class was in month of July, *červenec*, when the fruit ripens. January is *leden*, named after ice. November is *listopad*, for the falling leaves. March is *březen*, the month of pregnancy. May is *květen*, named for the flowers. August is *srpen*, the scythe of the harvest. February is *únor*, from the verb for plunging; or, as my teacher called it, the month of weary exhaustion.

k.

Dear B.,

These are the things I remember from four weeks of Czech class, a few days and months and numbers. I still can't read your letters or even order a meal, but I know that Sunday is *neděle*, the day of doing nothing. And Monday is *pondělí*, the day after the day of doing nothing.

k.

Dear B.,

I'd had too many days of doing nothing. I knew it was time to do something. Not an affair; I owed our marriage that much. But what?

k.

Dear B.,

After class on Wednesday (*středa*, the middle day), I took a train with classmates to the Sedlec Ossuary, the Bone Church. We arrived at the Kutná Hora station, about an hour from Prague, and rode in a bus through a *panelak* complex of Soviet era apartments. A teenaged couple boarded the bus and sat in front of me. Her head resting on his shoulder, her magenta hair cascading over her jacket, her fingers clutching his thick blond hair.

I thought of the young love of Kristla and Míla. Of Bára and the huntsman. Of Viktorka and the soldier. Of me and my husband: we were young lovers once. Maybe the couple on the bus would have a happy ending, or maybe they were already doomed.

k.

Dear B.,

This is not the book I meant to write about Prague. In that book, which I started years before this one, an American woman wants love but not marriage. All of her friends are getting married and she's in her thirties and marriage is what one, what everyone, does. Unless one goes to Prague instead.

k.

Dear B.,

Everyone says your life was bitter. But your endings, they say, were happy. Though *Babička* ends with the grandmother's death, the last line proclaims: *Šťastná to žena*—Happy woman!

The endings of the stories I write are unhappy by a ratio of twelve to two. The editor of my first book told me so. At a reading I gave in Texas, a student in the audience asked why all my female characters were crazy and depressed. At Thanksgiving, having read my book, my aunt said, "I thought you were such a happy person!"

k.

Dear B.,

Why are you sad? Kafka writes in the left margin of a letter to Milena, who was unhappily married to someone else. Again in the left margin of the next letter: *And why are you sad?*

k.

Dear B.,

In Czech class, one of the older Russians, Evgeny, and I were assigned to be dialogue partners practicing possessive pronouns. We were told we were a husband and wife—*manžel a manželka*—in the process of getting a divorce. We had to create a dialogue about who was going to get what. *Ta jachta je jeho*; the yacht is his. *Ten dům je můj*; the house is mine. *To auto je jeho*; the car is his. *Ten diamant je můj*; the diamond is mine. *To dítě je naše*; we shared the kid.

A year later, I would begin the same process—in Indiana, in English.

k.

Jste manžel a manželka Konec – finish.

to dítě – child To dítě je naše.
ta jachta – yacht Ta jachta je jeho. (EVGENY)
ten dům Ten dům je můj.
to auto To auto je jeho. (
ten diamant Ten diamant je můj

Practicing

Dear B.,

I secretly snapped a picture of the young lovers on the bus. The bus's digital clock is in the top right. Are they still in love? Maybe all that matters is that they were in love one summer's day at 16:28.

k.

Dear B.,

At the Sedlec Ossuary, the Bone Church, I felt lucky to be alive. Lucky to have my bones inside of my skin instead of in piles. Forty thousand people dead from the plague (not a happy ending), and no more room in the cemetery. So they—the people, their five-hundred-year-old bones—were made into a macabre monument. In the center hangs a chandelier made of bones. Candles rise from the tops of skulls set amid petals of pelvic bones. Femurs dangle like long rows of pipe chimes. Jawbones at the top, hundreds of them, wide open.

k.

Lucky

Love at 16:28

The plague

Dear B.,

In her final days, my Granny's jaw grew slack. Her false teeth were removed because she was no longer eating. Her lips and tongue dry. She communicated with a slow blink of her eyes. *Yes, I'm thirsty.* My mom dipped a lollipop stick topped with a soft sponge into a small cup of water and placed it in Granny's mouth so she could drink.

k.

Dear B.,

The Bone Church artist, František Rint, was from Česká Skalice. He was a friend of the Steidlers, who owned the inn where you danced. Maybe you knew him. Surely he knew you. He started work on the church shortly before you died and finished in 1870.

A hundred years later in 1970 the Czech Surrealist artist Jan Švankmajer made a short film of the church in black and white with frenetic cuts. There is the constant clicking of a bike chain turning (like clocks ticking), the coughing of a child as a guide tells the church's history. We never see the guide or the students—just rapid cuts of bone chandelier, bone shield, bone bird—but over and over, according to the subtitles, the guide tells the children, "Don't touch!"

k.

Dear B.,

The Bone Church is full of ghosts. They whisper in my ear when I take a photo: *Soon enough,* they say, *you too.* When I pose, the skulls smile behind me. I can hear them: *We once had flesh too.*

Kafka said: *Writing letters is an intercourse with ghosts, with one's own ghost, which secretly evolves in the letter one is writing.*

From my ghost to yours,
k.

Ghosts

Dear B.,

One night when your Grandmother is out doing an errand she hears something: young Kristla gathering leaves for her St. John's wreath, which she will place under her pillow in hopes of seeing her beloved Míla in a dream.

Many years earlier the Grandmother made a similar wreath and was given a vision of her husband, Jiří, now long dead, killed in the war. *How long, Jiří*, she says to the night, *How long?*

k.

Dear B.,

I was in Indiana when my grandfather, Grumpus, died in January 2012, a week before my grandparents' seventieth anniversary. They had been high school sweethearts, the match made by their conspiring sisters.

Five months later I drove ten hours to Elk Mountain, Pennsylvania; I wasn't going to miss Granny's death too. My mom read aloud the letters my grandfather had written in the 1940s when he was a soldier stationed in India: *I sure do miss you, sweetheart. Counting the days till we can be together again.*

k.

Dear B.,

I married my high school sweetheart. I asked him to the Sadie Hawkins dance. We hardly knew each other; the match was made by my conspiring friends who called him and pretended to be me, asking him to call me back. He called. I knew they had tricked us, but I knew I had to do it, to ask him to the dance, and I told myself, if he says no then years from now you will forget all about this moment, and if he says yes then years from now you will marry him, and I asked him to the dance and he said yes.

k.

Dear B.,

Nothing can come of it, says Rilke of young love, *nothing, that is, but disappointment.*

k.

Dear B.,

One of our Czech vocabulary words was the verb *tancovat*, to dance. In our workbooks we completed the Czech sentences: *Na zahradě Tomas a Ana* _____. In the garden Tomas and Ana _____. I knew I was supposed to use the other verb we had learned: to walk. I was supposed to say that Tomas and Ana walk in the garden. But I wrote *tancujou*: they dance. It's what I would want to do with Tomas in the garden.

k.

Dear B.,

The last week of class when I finally went to Česká Skalice, where you grew up, I didn't need my Czech dictionary to translate the second line of the sign on the outside wall of your museum:

Zde Na Jiřinkové Slavnosti
Tančila Božena Němcová
1837 A 1844.

I knew it said that here, you had danced.

k.

Dear B.,

At the Sadie Hawkins dance we danced and danced. After the dance we danced and kissed. Many nights after that we danced, at my house, in the dark, to songs on my dad's record player. And I knew I had been right that I would marry him.

k.

Dear B.,

Young people often err, says Rilke, *since it is their nature to be impatient.*

But what is to follow? What should fate do if this takes root, this heap of half-broken things that they call togetherness and that they would like to call their happiness?

k.

Dear B.,

What followed: Years after that first dancing date, after a series of break-ups and make-ups, we were finished with college and still together, together again. His co-worker advised him: "Dude, shit or get off the pot."

k.

Dear B.,

He proposed on Valentine's Day. There are two types of people in the world, B: those who propose marriage on Valentine's Day and those who, upon realizing a ring is about to appear before the main course, say, "Not now!" only to accept the proposal after dinner and later complain about getting engaged on that most obvious of days.

k.

Dear B.,

I saw very early, you wrote to your sister about your husband, *that our natures were not suited for each other.*
You wrote that when you got married, you cried your first bitter tears.

k.

Dear B.,

When I got married, I cried. My in-laws were worried. Why did she cry? But I always cry. I cried, I explained, because I cry.

k.

Dear B.,

But she won't cry, I wrote in one of my early short stories, set at a five-year-old's Chuck E. Cheese birthday party. *Not about her in-laws or about the other mothers or about the birthday girl's father (who had always and simply been wrong).*

k.

Dear B.,

I wish I could appreciate things like Valentine's Day. It would have been much easier on him. In my Chuck E. Cheese story, the husband accuses the wife of making everything more complicated than it needs to be. I identify with the wife, but I sympathize with the husband.

k.

Dear B.,

At the antique store with all the clocks, the man behind the counter looked to be about my age, but who knows when so much time is ticking. "*Dobrý den*," he said when I walked in. "*Dobrý den*," I answered. I am good at saying *dobrý den*, hello, good day. I say it with the Czech inflection, the lilting music of it. It's one of the few things I say well. So people often mistake me for someone who can actually speak Czech. They follow with a Czech question: "Can I help you? Are you looking for anything in particular?" But I panic, uncomprehending, and have to say, as I did to the man at the antique shop, "*Bohužel, nemluvím česky*." Unfortunately, I don't speak Czech.

k.

Dear B.,

Fortunately, he spoke some English. "*Mluvíte anglicky?*" I asked. "A little," he said, which of course meant a lot. "Do you love antiques?" I asked, revealing too much of my romance for them. He shrugged. It was his father's store, he said, and now it was his. He had studied philosophy at the university but it didn't get him a job. So here he was, behind the counter in an antique shop with dozens of clocks ticking away his life. "I work at a university," I told him. "I teach literature and writing." He asked about my job in a way that made me think he had his own romance with university positions. I shrugged. After six years on the tenure clock, I felt like I had a life sentence. "How can you endure these clocks ticking all day?" I asked.

k.

Dear B.,

It was said that your marriage was a failure from the very beginning. But marriages don't fail; people fail. Or: marriages don't fail; they end, like everything else. Or: they last, almost seventy years in the case of my grandparents, until death. But lasting is not the same as succeeding. You died before you could officially divorce. Lasting, I've often thought, is just a race with death. Which will end first, the marriage or the life? Tick, tick, tick.

k.

Dear B.,

The antique store guy said that you get used to it, the ticking. I looked up. The clocks were lined up along the twelve-foot high walls, all counting different seconds.

k.

Dear B.,

I get used to it, my husband sang in one of his songs back when he wrote songs. *That's all.* We agreed on what music to listen to, we shared parenting duties, and we both often felt awkward in our roles as parents. But we disagreed about politics and religion and what movies our daughter should watch and about whether I should get a Ph.D. and whether I should take a job in Indiana, whether he would (pretty please?) come to Prague with me, and whether Valentine's Day is an appropriate day to get engaged.

k.

Dear B.,

I had become, over the years, obsessed with what looked like happy marriages. Were they all secretly unhappy too? Sometimes I convinced myself they were, that we all were unhappy. If I was wrong, if some people were truly happy, it meant happiness in marriage was possible.

I also became obsessed with unhappy marriages. Like yours.

k.

Dear B.,

Then I saw it: a typewriter. It was only six hundred crowns, about thirty dollars. But I didn't know how I would get it home in my luggage or how to navigate the post office to ship it and suddenly I felt too intimate talking with this man about clocks and philosophy and universities and he was looking at me expectantly and all I wanted to do was leave. Was he interested in me? I'd been married so long I had no idea how to tell.

k.

Dear B.,

We had a fairy tale beginning, my husband and I. Did I mention the stars? Sixteen-years-old and a sky full of shooting stars. Oh how we danced. But that was once upon a time.

k.

Dear B.,

Prague is a fairy tale city. In "Divá Bára," Elška describes Prague: *Oh, Bára, dear, it is so beautiful there that you cannot even picture it in imagination. When I saw the Vltava, the beautiful churches, the huge buildings, the parks—I was as if struck dumb.*

In Prague the couples are all happily ever after. Couples on the long escalators down to the metro. Couples in the tram. Window shopping on Wenceslas Square. Walking along Charles Bridge. White peacocks roam the grounds at the Wallenstein Palace in Malá Strana, and couples don't even notice because they have each other.

k.

Dear B.,

Prague is a fairy tale. Happiness is a heap of half-broken things. The correct verb is not to dance but to walk. And once upon a time is always the beginning of an elaborate lie.

k.

Dear B.,

In 2010 my daughter was thirteen, and I took her abroad for the first time, to Prague. We kept having the same conversation in which I tried to get her to read Kafka's *The Metamorphosis* and she lobbied to "get a Facebook." We were staying in Vinohrady, not far from where Kafka is buried. According to my map, the cemetery was just past the mall, where I had taken her shopping to reward her for enduring a three-hour Communism tour given by a seventy-year-old man who had lived through all forty years of Czech Communism and who described events in a thick Czech accent that even I, who knew most of the history, struggled to understand. I'd thus far failed to get her to read *The Metamorphosis*, but I tried to lure her into a more active encounter: "Will you help me find Kafka's grave?"

k.

Can I get a Facebook?

Dear B.,

We took the tram to the mall and walked a block to the cemetery. Inside, the more we wandered, the bigger it grew. German graves, Czech graves. Gothic fonts, Art Nouveau fonts. Serifs and sans. It occurred to me that we would find Kafka in a German section. But after dozens of angels and crucifixes, I realized he would be in a Jewish section, that the language would be Hebrew. Wait, where were we, and where was the Jewish Cemetery?

k.

Where were we?

The fonts

Dear B.,

We were in Olšany Cemetery, searching—I later learned—for one single grave amid 65,000 tombstones across one hundred acres of land. The cemetery is a necropolis of twelve interconnected cemeteries, established in 1680 as a burial site for victims of the plague, and was used for another plague in 1787. Thus sayeth *Wikipedia*. Two million people have been buried in Olšany over the centuries, and we were searching for one grave.

"This is what one might call Kafkaesque," I said to my daughter, "if one had read any Kafka."

k.

Dear B.,

Yesterday I found the grave, Kafka wrote to Milena of her relative's grave in Prague. *If you look for it timidly it's really almost impossible to find it. I spent a long time there, the grave is beautiful, so indestructible in its stone.*

k.

Dear B.,

We didn't find Kafka's grave, not that year anyway. A few days later we went to yours, not in Olšany but in the National Cemetery at Vyšehrad. I've been there lots of times, taking the same picture over and over. We had to wait because there was already a couple standing at the foot of your grave, quiet. Instead of feeling happy that someone else knew you, I felt territorial. "What are *they* doing there?" I whispered to my daughter when we turned the corner. Like you are my secret.

k.

Secret

Dear B.,

Vyšehrad is one of my favorite places in Prague, with the remains of the original tenth-century fortified castle, the vistas up and down the Vltava, the quiet park space and the statues of Czech heroes including Princess Libuše, pointing toward Prague, Praha, the threshold. Because, she said, even kings must bow before a threshold.

Vyšehrad's National Cemetery is full of Prague's writers and artists. Across from you are Jan Neruda and Josef Frič, and down the same wall is Alphonse Mucha. Keep walking and there's Antonín Dvořák, Bedřich Smetana, Karel Čapek, and Karel Macha.

Your husband is buried far away in Tábor.

k.

Dear B.,

Whereas Václav Havel—who was a writer and dissident long before he became President of Czechoslovakia—is buried beside his wife Olga in the cemetery where I searched for (and three years later found) Kafka's grave.

Like you, Havel wielded his pen to fight for personal and political freedom. After the Soviet invasion that ended Prague Spring in August 1968, he was monitored by the secret police—like you and your husband were after 1848. In 1977 he co-authored *Charter 77*, a samizdat manifesto of protest and resistance, and was eventually and repeatedly imprisoned.

k.

Dear B.,

When I attended the Prague Summer Program in 2005, the writer Ivan Klíma was a guest speaker. In a large lecture room at Charles University, he described what it was like to write and type multiple copies of literary and political documents to circulate underground. He passed around—to a roomful of hungover American students!—a samizdat copy of Havel's *The Beggar's Opera*, and I got to hold it in my hands.

k.

Dear B.,

That was 2005, the year of Czech literature and beer. My professor Petr said that your image was used as the model for the Virgin Mary that was painted in the Týn Cathedral in Old Town Square. Class was held in his oversized office, and we sat on couches as he smoked and told us about Prague as a palimpsest. He led us on literary walking tours and started most of his sentences with, "Hokay, guys." One day he met us in the university's basement cafeteria so we could order beer to drink during class. His office was on the top floor of Charles University with views of the Prague Castle from his multiple windows. He let us climb out the windows and stand on the edge of the roof.

k.

Dear B.,

For years my marriage was a heap of half-broken things, but I kept it to myself. It seemed I even kept it *from* myself, a form of protection. I didn't think I ever wrote, even to myself, about how I really felt, but there is this in my typed journal from my trip to Prague in 2005 about the emails my husband and I exchanged:

I think of our emails that are just like our life together—which is to say, apart. Everything's just down to business, no sense or questioning of what's going on inside each other. No interest. No connection. And I think: something's wrong.

k.

Dear B.,

Havel wrote letters to his wife Olga during his longest stint in prison, 1979 to 1983. He told her that he passed the time reading George Sand, the Bible, Dickens, Drieser, London, even Harper Lee. He dreamed of Miloš Forman (*Miloš has been haunting me in my dreams*), pondered the death of John Lennon (*his death so compellingly reaches beyond itself*), and invoked Kafka (*Today I see prison as an authentically absurd experience, one that every careful reader of Kafka should understand well*).

k.

Dear B.,

Havel asked Olga to send him cigarettes, juices, sweets, toothpaste, lotions, vitamin C, soap, a 1980 calendar, and, most of all, he wanted letters from her. But early on it was clear that he would give more than he received in correspondence:

My dear Grumbler, I think of you with tenderness and I even accept with tenderness the fact that you don't write, that you don't do what I ask or respond to my letters (do you at least read them carefully?).

k.

Dear B.,

Kafka was so grateful when Milena's letters arrived that he couldn't help but repeat himself:

The telegram, thanks, thanks, thanks. I read and re-read it and couldn't come to the end of my joy and gratitude.

So beautiful, so beautiful, Milena, so beautiful...the writing of letters.

Such short, gay or at least spontaneous letters as these two of today, this is already almost (almost, almost, almost, almost) forest and wind in your sleeves.

Yours, yours, yours,
k.

Dear B.,

Bohumil Hrabal wrote letters to an American woman named April. He called her Dubenka because *duben*, oak leaf, is the Czech word for April.

He called his favorite cat Cassius.

I rattle out of the typewriter the pages of these letters—only Cassius knows, I whisper to him, that I love you. But you don't expect one from me, since I don't send these letters.

k.

Dear B.,

A year before he died, Grumpus asked me to follow him as he wheeled his walker down the hallway to his bedroom. I sat on the edge of the bed and watched him remove a cardboard box from a shelf. He put the box in my hands. "I don't know what to do with this, honey," he said, crying his Slavic tears, the ones that flowed freely ever since his first stroke. "They're letters that Marge and I wrote during the war. I should probably just throw them away or burn them. But you're a writer. Maybe you know what to do with them." Now I was crying too. "We were just kids then," he said. "We didn't know anything."

k.

You're a writer

Dear B.,

I read an article that was an ode to sadness: how powerful it is, how it inspires us to wrestle and create, how it is the source of so much of the art that we love and the reason that we love it.

You wrote *Babička* after the death of your fifteen-year-old son Hynek. (In 2012 my daughter was fifteen.) You were so filled with grief that you turned to memories of your childhood. And you were so filled with heartache from your own love life that you wrote love stories with happy endings. The Grandmother intercedes for Kristla and Míla, and they are finally married. She also intercedes for the Countess who loves her painting teacher instead of the Count to whom she is betrothed.

k.

Dear B.,

But even underneath or in the left margin of your *Šťastná to žena*—happy woman!—there is always sadness. The Countess should have lived happily ever after. She married her beloved art teacher, and they moved away and had a baby. The story should have ended there: happily ever after. But within two years the Countess was dead.

The Grandmother says that God takes those he loves best when they are happiest. God's idea of a happy ending.

k.

Dear B.,

Bohumil Hrabal's idea of a happy ending: In *Too Loud a Solitude*, the narrator, Hanta, spends his life working at a paper compacter so that he can save his favorite books from destruction. He fills his small apartment floor to ceiling with books. But when his machine is going to be replaced by a modern facility, Hanta crawls into the paper compacter to be crushed with his beloved books. It's my favorite book.

k.

Dear B.,

In the cold first month, *leden* (ice), of 2012 I called my mom who was caring for my grandparents, and she said Grumpus was unresponsive. She said, "It's like he's in a coma, not eating or waking up. The nurse says he could wake up, but come on, he's ninety." Mom said it was probably the end. The last conversation they'd had was about his teeth. His mouth was bothering him, so she took his teeth and cleaned them. "I've had three cosmos," Mom continued. "Do you want a kitten? I have the sweetest kitten and I can't let her inside because of my allergies. It's going to be five degrees tonight. We need someone to write the obituary," she said, taking another sip of her cosmo. "I'm not a good writer." But she was wrong; she's a great writer. I have thought so many times while reading her email updates. "I can do it if you want, Mom," I said. Six hundred miles away, I made a cosmo too.

k.

Dear B.,

When Granny could no longer walk to the bathroom even with her walker, my mom and uncle put a portable potty next to her recliner in the family room. Once when she was using the toilet in the middle of the room, she asked about my grandfather. "Where's John?"

My mother pointed to the box of his ashes on the fireplace. "He's up there, Mom."

"Oh, that figures," Granny said from her toilet. "He's always got to keep an eye on me, even when I go to the bathroom."

k.

Dear B.,

When your Grandmother is dying, she gets confused and calls for her oldest granddaughter Barunka, the character named for you. But Barunka was not there. *Is she happy?* The Grandmother asks.

When I went to be with my dying Granny, I'm glad she didn't ask if I was happy.

k.

Dear B.,

It was 2012, the year of you. What I felt was fragments and half-broken things, my dead grandparents, time ticking. The sadness of beginning my own unhappy ending.

k.

Dear B.,

In Czech class we practiced writing postcards. I wrote to my daughter: *Pozdrav z Prahy. Mám se dobře. Studuju čestinu kazdy den na letní škole.* Greetings from Prague. I'm fine. I study Czech every day at the language school. And: *Stýská se me.* I miss you.

k.

Dear B.,

Sometimes the only thing people write on a postcard is: *Jsem tam.* I am there.

k.

Jsem tam

Dear B.,

Two of the Russians in my Czech class, Svetlana and Ekatarina, constantly interrupted the teacher, scratching the air with overlong fingernails, calling out, "*Mám otázku! Mám otázku!*" I have a question! My partner Valerie and I kept a daily tally of how many times they interrupted with another *otázku*, rolling our eyes each time. Svetlana usually won.

k.

Dear B.,

It was 2012 and your hometown had officially declared it *Rok Boženy Němcové*, The Year of Božena Němcová. I skipped class and took a two-hour train from Prague to Česká Skalice. The woman at the station's info booth didn't speak English, but she pointed toward a sign with your name on it. I wandered up a hill and through the town's unpopulated streets, searching. Eventually I encountered two bicyclists who had stopped to check their maps. I used my three-and-a-half weeks of Czech to ask them, "*Prosím, nevíte kde je Muzeum Boženy Němcové?*" But no, they did not know where your museum was. I showed them my map, and tried a different approach: "*Kde jsme?*" Where are we? But they didn't know that either.

k.

Dear B.,

I spotted an old woman in her garage painting a chair and could not help but think of your Grandmother. I needed to get her attention and said the first thing that came to mind: "*Mám otázku!*"

I understood as she pointed *tam*, there, and then *doleva*, left, and then *doleva* again, and then *na prava*, it's on the right. I understood that it would take about *deset minut*, 10 minutes. And there you were.

I walked straight to your statue, in the small green space outside the museum. "I made it," I told you.

k.

Kde jsme?

291

I made it

Dear B.,

Outside the Muzeum Boženy Němcové a few women were smoking, their leashed dog waiting patiently. Inside, as outside in the town, I seemed to be the only one there. The first room, spacious and lined with windows like a grade school cafeteria, was filled with pieces of you: your family tree, your son's artwork, your dead husband (literally: a picture of him dead). Behind glass: your cloak, your pen, a lock of your hair. I signed the guest book so everyone would know: *jsem tam.* I am there.

k.

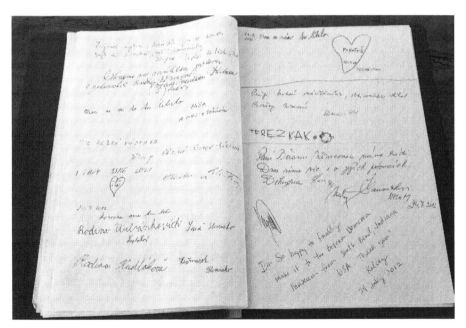

I'm so happy

Dear B.,

The museum went on and on. Upstairs was a series of rooms with paintings of you, a statue, a bust, your books in different languages and by different illustrators, pictures of the houses and towns you'd lived in, images of dramatizations of your works. Costumes and photos from stage productions.

Then the hall where you danced, crowned Queen of the Dahlia Ball. The walls were pale green, the pillars mahogany. The room was quiet and empty except for a few chairs facing a small stage with a piano and cello. Sunlight fell through the windows onto the parquet floor. I walked through the room slowly, thinking, *Here, Božena Němcová danced.* Thinking, *I am there.*

k.

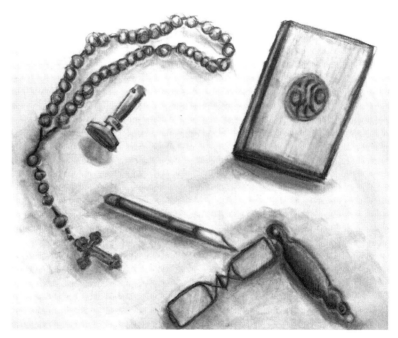

Pieces of you

Here, Božena Němcová danced

Dear B.,

I knew by now, in my final week of class, that I wasn't going to learn enough Czech to read your letters without unlimited time and dictionaries. But in your museum, in front of your cloak, on the dance floor, beside your statue, pressed against the door of the church where you were married, I felt like I was getting to know you better.

k.

Dear B.,

But I had more to know. I asked a woman at the front desk how to get to Ratibořice, where I knew I would find the castle in *Babička*, along with *Babiččino údolí,* Grandmother's Valley. Specifically I asked her how to find a bus to take me there. She spoke three-fourths Czech, one-fourth English, and I spoke the reverse. She shook her head, confused. She said there was a—"how do you say?"—nature path. That I had to walk by foot. Czechs have one verb for going somewhere by transportation (*jet*) and another for going by foot (*jít*). So they often say you have to walk by foot. Walk by foot? It was over three kilometers! My feet had already walked that far to get to the museum. "*Ano,*" she said. Yes.

Exhaustedly yours,
k.

Walk by foot

Dear B.,

And so, for several kilometers, I walked by foot through woods, along an open field, no one in sight. Hoping I was not as lost as I felt, thinking this would be a good place for a trail of breadcrumbs. The only signs were names of flowers and birds in Czech: *kukačka, žluva, žluna, puštik, červenka.* But the cuckoo, oriole, woodpecker, owl, and robin were not going to help.

k.

Birds of Bohemia

Dear B.,

At the castle, I found a young man who spoke English, and he explained that his next tour was starting soon, but that it would be in Czech. I followed along with the group, reading a printed English script while he explained everything in Czech. Each room was named for its function: the Entrance Hall, the Reception Salon, Salon of the Three Emperors, Ladies Salon, etc. Twice the tour guide addressed me in English. Once to tell me what he had already said in Czech: I was not permitted to stand outside the rug; and once to tell me, since he knew I was interested, that I was in the Chamber of the Princess, where your famous scene of the Granny's visit with the Princess is set. Where, if rumors about the princesses are true, you may have been conceived.

k.

Dear B.,

Max Brod believed that Kafka's *The Castle* was inspired by your portrayal of this one in *Babička*.

I read *The Castle* in grad school, 2003, just after my first trip to Prague, where I'd toured the Prague Castle and visited Kafka's tiny house on Golden Lane.

Back in the U.S., my classmates spoke of Kafka's castle as a metaphor for God, for self, for the unattainable, and I kept thinking no, it's real, the castles in Europe are everywhere and real.

k.

Dear B.,

After the tour I continued to walk the grounds, through woods and clearings, past the Old Bleachery, the mill where the Prošek family lived and worked in *Babička*, past the fields where both Barunka the character and you as Barunka the child would have roamed. Eventually I arrived at the famous statue of the Grandmother and the children in Grandmother's Valley. By now it was late afternoon and I had to retrace all those kilometers to the train station and ride two hours to Prague, and perhaps this moment should have been the climactic culmination of my getting-to-know-you, but the fact is I was hungry and tired and seriously afraid of getting lost on the way back.

yours anyway,
k.

This moment

Dear B.,

I returned to Czech class the next day. I hadn't told anyone that I'd be gone, and when we started class with our conversation practice, Evgeny started the discussion by asking me where I'd been the day before. Most classes began like this: *How are you? What did you eat for breakfast? What did you do this weekend?* Often I made up answers because I didn't know how to say what I actually ate or did. But it was the final week and I finally could put together a basic sentence in past tense. So when Evgeny asked me, *Kde jste se včera?* I answered, *Jel jsem do České Skalice.*

And then he said, as we had learned from our postcards: *Stýská se mi po Kelcey.* I missed Kelcey. The class nodded in agreement.

And I realized: I'd missed them too.

k.

Dear B.,

It's late, and I'm reading Bohumil Hrabal's *Total Fears*, his book of letters to Dubenka:

And at home I found the ending of the third part of T.S. Eliot's The Waste Land *and I read it to the moon from the fifth floor.*

Božena, I'm writing to you about reading Hrabal who was writing to Dubenka about reading T.S. Eliot to the moon.

k.

Dear B.,

Hrabal wrote, in 1989, about getting older, about remembering: *I who have aged so much now that I live and feed off childhood memories.*

He remembered his childhood room, always filled with sunlight. He remembered the bed he was born in, the same one where his grandfather died.

He remembered his grandmother as she picked tomatoes and beans: *I was simply there with granny, always bathed in sunlight, even if it started to drizzle.*

k.

Dear B.,

Hrabal wrote, in 1989, about the previous August 21, the twentieth anniversary of the Russian tanks rolling into Prague in 1968, about the end of Prague Spring, about the end of the period of possibility, about *all those fine young men who emigrated:* Milan Kundera, Miloš Forman, Jáchym Topol.

It's so sad, Dubenka.

k.

All those fine young men

Dear B.,

He wrote of his "Slav propensity to tears":

I know, Dubenka, the heroes of Dostoyevsky novels also like to weep a lot, with their mild cholera, induced by the drink. Actually I've got mild cholera too, just like Dostoyevsky did.

k.

Dear B.,

And Hrabal wrote, in 1989, about suicide, about falling or jumping from a fifth-story balcony, about all the authors who killed themselves, about how he didn't kill himself, he just went to the pub. He wrote about pigeons and doves and how they filled the public spaces in Prague until the government stopped letting people feed them.

And then, in 1997, while feeding pigeons, Hrabal fell from a fifth-story window and died.

k.

Dear B.,

When I arrived in Slovakia in 2012, my relatives greeted me with a shot of *slivovitz*, plum brandy, and fed me a homemade dinner of a chicken they had just killed in the yard. They drove me to the next relative's house, where we drank another shot. The next day, we went from family home to family home—one like an Ikea display model, one cabin off a rural road, two Soviet prefab apartments—from *slivovitz* to *slivovitz*. On Sunday morning at 7:30 a.m., Marta, the only English speaker, told me to dress for church. Her brother Josef poured me a shot and we toasted, *Na zdravie!* We walked to the fifteenth-century Gothic church where my great-grandmother had been baptized and sat in the back. I brought home souvenirs: a half-dozen shot glasses wrapped in leather with a strap to be worn around the neck. Etched in the leather wrap: *Nech žije kto pije.* Long live those who drink.

k.

Na zdravie

Dear B.,

Surrounded by the High Tatra Mountains, Okoličné is in the Liptov region, which you visited to record folk tales. You wrote that the area was an immense treasure that no one really cared about except to travel through. Which must be why my relatives smiled when I said your name.

k.

Health

Dear B.,

Sixty kilometers to the west, in 1921, Kafka stayed in a sanatorium to revive his health. A few years earlier, as WWI was breaking out in Europe, my great-grandparents packed everything and left for the U.S., where they soon had four children. They spoke to my grandfather and his older sisters in Slovak, and the children replied in English. My grandfather's beloved sister Amelia died at age 17 of tuberculosis. He and his other sisters Sue and Martha each lived more than ninety years. All dead now.

k.

All dead now

Dear B.,

I met my grandfather's ninety-year-old first cousin, Paul, whom my grandfather never met, and who lived with his wife in the house where my great-grandmother was born. I couldn't stop crying; he reminded me so much of Grumpus. Paul looked me in the eyes and spoke in long Slovak paragraphs, then waited patiently while his niece Marta translated: "For four months," *štyri mesiac*, he said, and this bit of Slovak I actually understood from Czech class: *čtyři měsíc*, "we had to live in the cellar. The soldiers came and took over the house and we were made prisoners in our own home."

He had never met me, but he wanted me to know this injustice from the war. The other thing he wanted me to know: that he still writes his wife poetry just like when they met.

k.

Poetry

Dear B.,

Rilke to the young poet: *Can you avow that you would die if you were forbidden to write?*

Above all, in the most silent hour of your night, ask yourself this: Must I write?

Avowedly,
k.

Dear B.,

The writer Karolina Světlá said of you:
She wanted to live only by the pen.

k.

Dear B.,

In 2012, I rented an apartment on Kolinská street from a woman named Renata. I arrived jet-lagged and luggage-less, awake in the middle of my U.S. night, greeted by a bright blond woman in a purple and white apartment. I didn't have access to a phone so Renata called her Czech boyfriend in Cape Cod who told me how to set up Viber so the airport could call me when my luggage arrived. Renata asked about me. "I'm a professor," I told her. (One never admits to being a writer.) "And you?" I asked. "A writer," she said. "A writer?" I said. "A writer." Renata the Writer showed me her web page. On the web page, a best-selling book: *Climbing to the Top: Strategies for Success from Those Who Know.* On the cover of the best-selling book: a picture of Renata.

k.

Dear B.,

One morning before Czech language class I was watching *Dobre Rano!—Good Morning!*—the local morning TV show and there, on Renata's TV, was Renata the Writer. She was being interviewed about her best-selling book. The caption described her as: *kouč, spisovatelka, a školitelka*. Coach, writer, and trainer.

k.

Dear B.,

At the Shakespeare a Synové bookstore in Malá Strana I snapped a picture of a picture: A smiling *spisovatelka*, Milena Oda, holding up a copy of her book. She is wearing black pants and a white t-shirt that says: I AM A WRITER NOT A FUCKING BESTSELLER.

k.

Dear B.,

You were a writer—*spisovatelka*—and a bestseller. But you were a bestseller too late. You died begging friends for food and money.

k.

Spisovatelka

Dear B.,

All I am is literature, Kafka says, *and I am not able or willing to be anything else.*

Everything that is not literature bores me.

k.

Dear B.,

Hrabal told Dubenka the reason he didn't sign *Charter 77*, even when Václav Havel showed up at the Golden Tiger pub and asked him in person: *I wouldn't swap that signature for my* Too Loud a Solitude. *I mean, Dubenka, the only purpose of my being in this world has been to write this* Too Loud a Solitude.

k.

Dear B.,

Havel went to prison for the documents he signed.

He told Olga in a postscript: *I'm going through a period now when I don't like anything I've ever written and it worries me that I haven't written more and better. I wonder what will come of it? Here I will write nothing, that much is clear by now; it's simply impossible.*

But he was wrong. In prison he wrote and he wrote.

k.

Dear B.,

And you. You wrote to your sister: *As if by a miracle, poetry awakened me to life in my unhappiness! It sweetens my life, and I have consecrated myself to it for all eternity!*

k.

Dear B.,

Your husband did not wish you to be a writer. My husband did not wish me to be a writer either. There were things I didn't wish about him too. We both let each other do the things we did not wish each other to do; we gave each other space and time, swapped kid duties, and wished each other luck. But we never wanted those things—the things we wanted most deeply for ourselves—for each other.

k.

Dear B.,

For as long as I knew them, my grandparents bickered and yelled and waged war on the volumes of their respective televisions (his in the living room, hers in the kitchen). They engaged in bumper-car battles with their walkers, fighting for the right of way in the hallway. She repeated indignities: "I was never good enough for his parents because I was Irish. And what was so special about Slovaks? His father didn't even know any English!" I learned it was all an extended battle over a long-ago betrayal.

k.

Dear B.,

But there's this, a letter from the box Grumpus gave me, a happy day from her to him:

January 16, 1945
40th letter
Dearest Johnny,
Happy anniversary darling. No matter where you are at this time I want you to hear me saying I love you so. This day means so much to me. To think I married the most wonderful man in the world. You are wonderful you know. All day I went through memories from the day we got married until now. I can picture everything so well. That day we said I do & you squeezed my hand as you said it and how funny you were trying to put my ring on me. That day was such a happy day.

k.

Dear B.,

Did my grandparents get a happy ending? It was the first week of 2012; he had been dying for days. Finally my mom and uncle wheeled Granny into his room and she held his hand and said, as they instructed her: "I forgive you, John." Then she said it again, louder. He was hard of hearing and she was used to having to repeat herself. "He's squeezing my hand," she said to my mom and uncle. It was the only sign of life he'd given all week, my mom told me later. "He won't let go," Granny said. My mom and uncle left my grandparents alone in the room. When they got back he was dead.

k.

Dear B.,

I was born in the USA, born in the USA, born in the USA, is what all the Czechs sang at the Springsteen concert. I took a tram to the Synot Stadium and bought a ticket for twelve hundred crowns from a British family. Springsteen started the concert with "The Ghost of Tom Joad," an ode to the last time he'd played in Prague in the nineties. I was far away from the USA. Surrounded by thousands of people, I was lonely and alone.

k.

Dear B.,

It was 2012, *Rok Boženy Němcové*, the year of you, and I was in Prague and it had been too many days of doing nothing. Too much fiction, too much silence.

Still it would be months before I would have the nerve to say, in a quiet post-Thanksgiving conversation over coffee, "Mom, I think it's over." My seventeen-year marriage.

I spoke it into existence, the beginning of the end.

k.

Fiction and silence

Dear B.,

He left. My husband. We agreed it would happen but it hardly seemed possible. And then it happened. It was spring 2013 and he packed the car full of a heap of half-broken things and drove from South Bend to Cincinnati. He would start over where we had come from.

When he left I cried. Before he left, I made him a sandwich and cried. The night before, we drank a beer and talked about his leaving, and I cried. But I never said, No, stop, don't leave.

k.

Dear B.,

I am also good at saying goodbye: *Na shledanou.*

k.

Dear B.,

That night, after my husband left, I played poker with some colleagues who played regularly at one of their homes. I had never joined them, and I didn't want to then, but I made myself go. I hadn't told any of them what was going on in my life because nothing had actually happened until that day.

That night, I sat next to the person I would soon fall in love with and I lost every hand and when I ran out of poker chips he gave me some of his and when he asked me what I did that day I said I graded papers.

k.

Dear B.,

I heard an interview on the radio with the writer Edna O'Brien. She said that when she was young and growing up on a farm, she read books and wished that all of life could be lived in that key: that heightened state of literature. So she became a writer.

It was 2013, my husband had left, and I began living in that key. Where everything aches but the windows are open again and the woodpecker hammers at the tree and the neighbor cuts his lawn and my daughter turns up the pop music in her room as she gets ready for her date.

k.

Dear B.,

And, but, suddenly: there was love.

Just like literature.

k.

And, but, suddenly

And letters, B—

Furious letters. Love letters. Life-sustaining letters. Samizdat letters. Like yours, like Kafka's, like Rilke's, like Havel's, like Hrabal's.

k.

Dear B.,

I already knew him, the person I fell in love with. We were colleagues, we were friends, we were both in other relationships. But we sometimes left music mixes in each other's faculty mailboxes. And when the other relationships ended, we were sitting next to each other at a game of poker.

k.

And lust, B—

There was lust like I thought was dried up and dead, strung up like a chandelier in a church of bones. Lust like the Vltava flooding the fucking city.

k.

Dear B.,

Rilke's fourth letter: *Physical lust is a sensuous experience. It is a glorious infinite experience granted us, a gift of knowledge from the world, the fullness and radiance of all knowing.*

Lust like a field of four-leaf clovers.

Love like literature. Letters like literature. Life like literature.

Lust like clocks ticking and ticking.

k.

Dear B.,

I could easily slip into romantic thoughts, you wrote to Ivan.

The moon shines with a full face into my windows, the fragrance blows pleasantly into my room, all around is silence, there is nothing lacking but the sound of a stage coach stopping under the windows.

k.

Dear B.,

I love the whole world, Kafka wrote to Milena after a secret meeting, *and this includes your left shoulder, no it was first the right one, so I kiss it if I feel like it (and if you are nice enough to pull the blouse away from it) and this also includes your left shoulder and your face above me in the forest and my resting on your almost bare breast.*

k.

Dear B.,

Actually, wrote Rilke, *the creative experience lies so unbelievably close to the sexual, close to its pain and its pleasure, that both phenomena are only different forms of the same longing and bliss.*

k.

Technically, B—

The letters were emails, but the word hardly seems to fit. Emails are what you get from your Associate Dean of Recruitment and Retention, what you get from Chase and Discover and Netflix, what you get from your mother when your grandparents are dying, what you get from your soon-to-be ex-husband telling you what a terrible human being you are, what you get from your lawyer with documents to sign.

Letters, B, are what you get from the person you are falling fast in love with before you've even finished telling your friends about your upcoming divorce and they, those letters, those words, are what sustain you when seeing him is nearly impossible. Letters are what you fall in love with.

k.

Dear B.,

Kafka wrote to Milena that her letters were *the most beautiful thing that ever happened to me in my life.*

k.

Dear B.,

Olga and I have not professed love for each other for at least two hundred years, Václav Havel said of his wife, *but we both feel that we are probably inseparable.*

k.

Dear B.,

Kafka asked Milena:
Won't you reach out your hand towards me over all this and leave it with me for a long, long time?

k.

Dear B.,

I finally got it: a Czech typewriter. A 1968 Consul. But I didn't get it in Prague; I got it on eBay, shipped from California to Indiana.

It was late 2013 and the first thing I did was type a note to my new love on the paper it was wrapped in. I borrowed lines from a Czech phrase book: *Mám tě rádo.* I like you. *Miluji tě.* I love you. *Dobrou noc.* Good night.

Then I typed your name over and over, accents and all.

k.

Ž, ě, and á!

Dear B.,

In your book *Karla a jiné povídky*, *Karla and Other Tales*, I found a piece of paper. Someone else had written your name over and over too.

k.

Dubská

Dear B.,

Your husband, whom no one remembers, once told you: "No one will ever remember you."

k.

Dear B.,

Because we were divorcing in Indiana and because we had a child, my soon-to-be-ex-husband and I were required to attend four parenting classes. One class reviewed the five stages of grief—denial, anger, bargaining, depression, acceptance—and that was when I realized: he was in the early stages. I was almost at the end; I'd been going through them for years.

k.

Dear B.,

For one human being to love another, wrote Rilke, *is perhaps the most difficult task of all, the epitome, the ultimate test. It is that striving for which all other striving is merely preparation.*

I had been striving and preparing for the difficult task the ultimate test the epitome for one human being.

believe me,
k.

Dear B.,

In the right-hand margin of a letter to Milena, Kafka wrote: *And in spite of everything I sometimes believe: If one can perish from happiness, then this must happen to me. And if a person designated to die can stay alive through happiness, then I will stay alive.*

k.

Dear B.,

This was not the book I meant to write about Prague. That book, the one I tried writing for years, was supposed to be a bestseller. With love affairs and plot twists, with a happy ending. But I didn't know how to write about love, not to mention happy endings.

k.

Dear B.,

You wrote about love as free and beautiful and open. You fought for happy endings for everyone. You loved and loved and loved. But still didn't get a happy ending.

k.

Dear B.,

It is 2016, and I am in Prague, and the man I am in love with is in Prague, and together we go to your grave, to your statue, and to the house where your *Grandmother* was born, where an old Czech man stops to tell us that you were a famous writer of fairy tales. We walk across the Charles Bridge and we kiss and I cry Slavic tears because I have never kissed anyone in Prague before and because it is a fairy tale, and I don't believe in fairy tales.

k.

Dear Božena, Mother of Czech Prose:

Mám otázku: Do I have to die now to get my happy ending?

k.

Or perhaps, B—

I can just stop here, now, in this moment, and this will be my happy ending.

always,
k.

Image Credits

All artwork and photos are by the author unless otherwise noted.

Title page

Ink drawing of Božena Němcová.

PART ONE: THE BITTER LIFE OF BOŽENA NĚMCOVÁ
1. Shrouded in Mystery

"Ratibořice Castle," personal photo.

Photos of Princess Kateřina Zaháňská, Božena Němcová, and Princess Dorothea Talleyrand, public domain.

"Queen of the Dahlia Ball," personal photo taken outside the Muzeum Boženy Němcové in Česká Skalice.

"Shrouded in mystery," collage of Němcová with acrylic, graphite, vintage postcard, and text from her correspondence.

"To where are they leading the maiden in the white dress?" acrylic, graphite, and collage.

"A dolorous 'I do,'" collage of Josef Němec portrait with personal photo of the church where he and Němcová were married. Text translates to lines from "Čtyry doby": "Through the church resounds a dolorous 'I do.' Oh bride, alas!"

"As though she wants to perish in the wild swirl," vintage Czech postcard, postmarked 1909, with collage figures taken from 1951 edition of Němcová's *Divá Bára*, illustrated by Karel Müller.

2. She Loved to Love

"What I wanted," photomontage of images from *Praha Objektivem Mistrů* (*Prague Through the Lens of the Masters*), edited by Ludvík Baran, Panorama, 1983.

"The moon shines with a full face," acrylic and collage on back cover of 1948 edition of *Babička*. Helcelet's portrait with Czech text of Němcová's letter to Helcelet, 29 July 1851.

"My miserable life," acrylic and collage of Klácel. Czech text translates to: "I consider the greatest treasure of my miserable life to be the favor of this Božena."

"The Brotherhood," acrylic and collage of Němcová and key members of the Czech-Moravian Brotherhood. From top to bottom: Helcelet, Klácel, Hanuš, Němec.

"He who gazes," collage portrait of Bendl with lines from his 1855 poem as published in *Výbor z korespondence Boženy Němcové*.

"Clouds everywhere, everywhere," acrylic and collage.

3. A Way of Life

"And the country folk!" vintage Czech postcard, dated 1905.

"Pictures from Slovakian life," vintage Czech postcard, undated.

"So many letters," images of Němcová on title page of 1917 *Výbor z korespondence Boženy Němcové*, purchased by the author for one hundred crowns (about five dollars).

"Kafka," personal photo of marker at Franz Kafka's birthplace in Prague's Old Town Square.

"Mr. Husband," collage of Josef Němec and Němcová's correspondence. Circled text translates to "Mr. Husband."

"Crowns," personal photo of Czech currency.

4. A Mode of Remembering

"What treasures," personal photo of plaque on Němcová's grave illustrating scene from *Babička*.

"And you might have been so happy!" erasure and translation of passage from 1948 edition of *Babička*.

"Sleep, my baby, sleep," acrylic and collage of Viktorka's lullaby.

"Death overtook her," erasure and translation of passage from 1948 edition of *Babička*.

"She lives on," watercolor and ink drawing of statue by Otto Gutfreund in "Granny's Valley," collaged on book cover of the 1948 edition of *Babička*.

"I see a great city whose glory will touch the stars," digitally altered personal photo of statue of Libuše and her husband Přemysl, collaged on acrylic background. The statue is located at Vyšehrad, site of Prague's first settlement and castle, and Libuše is pointing toward what is now central Prague, proclaiming her vision.

"Is she happy?" digitally altered personal photos of bust of Němcová layered over image of imprisoned Christians in the Statuary of St. John of Matha, St. Felix of Valois, and St. Ivan on Prague's Charles Bridge.

5. The Beautiful Star of Love

"We too were determined to 'devote ourselves to literature,'" personal photo of Jan Neruda's grave in the National Cemetery in Vyšehrad, located directly across from Němcová's grave.

"I am a woman, I am, I am," ink drawing with acrylic.

"Death came to her," acrylic, watercolor, ink, and found text.

"Grave," personal photo of Němcová's grave in Prague's National Cemetery.

"The beautiful star of love," acrylic and graphite on canvas with found text of a letter from Bendl to Němcová. Czech text translates to "poetry lives" or "poetry feeds."

PART TWO: POSTCARDS TO BOŽENA

"Tram from Vinohrady," vintage Czech postcard, postmarked 1909.

"Prague is young," personal photo of house on Ječná street in Prague where Němcová wrote *Babička*.

"Honor her memory," acrylic painting of plaque at Ječná house.

"Practicing," personal photo of author's notes from Czech class.

"Lucky," personal photo; used by permission of Sedlec Ossuary.

"Love at 16:28," acrylic painting.

"The plague," acrylic and ink painting of bones at Sedlec Ossuary.

"Ghosts," personal photo; used by permission of Sedlec Ossuary.

"Can I get a Facebook?" personal photo of author's daughter.

"Where were we?" photomontage of Prague street and Jewish Cemetery with images from *Praha Objektivem Mistrů*.

"The fonts," watercolor and ink painting.

"Secret," personal photo of Němcová's grave in Prague's National Cemetery.

"You're a writer," personal photo of letters written by author's grandparents in WWII.

"*Jsem tam*," vintage Czech postcard, postmarked 1909.

"*Kde jsme?*" acrylic and ink.

"I made it," personal photo.

"I'm so happy," personal photo.

"Pieces of you," graphite drawing.

"Here, Božena Němcová danced," acrylic and collage of outside wall of Steidler's Inn, current home of the Muzeum Boženy Němcové. The full text of the sign reads: "Here, at the Dahlia Ball, Božena Němcová danced in 1837 and 1844."

"Walk by foot," personal photo.

"Birds of Bohemia," watercolor, ink, and acrylic.

"This moment," personal photo of statue by Otto Gutfreund in "Granny's Valley."

"All those fine young men," photomontage of images from *Praha Objektivem Mistrů* and the December 7, 1968 issue of the Czech newspaper *Svět*.

"*Na zdravie*," personal photo of author, her cousin Josef, and *slivovitz*, taken in Okoličné, Slovakia.

"Health," personal photo of Okoličné, Slovakia.

"All dead now," family photo of author's great-grandparents, Michael and Susan (née Zuzka Sališ) Bobrovcan, surrounded by their children, John (later known as Grumpus), Amelia, Martha, and Susan. Taken in Hillside, New Jersey around 1930.

"Poetry," personal photo of cousin Paul and his wife, taken in their home in Okoličné, Slovakia. This is the home where the author's great-grandmother was born, and which the Russian soldiers occupied for four months during WWII.

"*Spisovatelka*," watercolor and ink.

"Fiction and silence," vintage Czech postcard, postmarked 1907, with collage figures taken from 1951 edition of Němcová's *Divá Bára*, illustrated by Karel Müller.

"And, but, suddenly," photomontage of images from *Praha Objektivem Mistrů*.

"Ž, ě, and á!" personal photo.

"1968 Consul," ink drawing.

"*Dubská*," personal photo of paper found in 1974 edition of Němcová's *Karla a jiné povídky*.

Sources and Works Consulted

"500 Czech Crown Banknote." *Prague.net.* n.d.

Baran, Ludvík. Ed. *Praha Objektivem Mistrů* (*Prague Through the Lens of the Masters*). Panorama, 1983.

Bažant, Jan, Nina Bažantová, and Frances Starn, eds. *The Czech Reader: History, Politics, Culture.* Duke UP, 2010.

Bowring, John. Trans. "Oldřich and Božena." *Cheskian Anthology: Being a History of the Poetical Literature of Bohemia.* R. Hunter, 1832.

"Božena Němcová." *Radio Prague's Virtual Cemetery.* Radio Prague, 1997.

"Božena Němcová." *Wikipedia.* n.d.

"Božena Němcová—*Babička.*" *Fortune City.* 2000.

Brod, Max. *Franz Kafka: A Biography.* Schocken Books, 1960.

Callow, John. "Sorceress of the Folk Spirits: Božena Němcová." Abstract. *Treadwell's Books.* 25 Feb 2008.

Cooper, David. "Mystifications and Ritual Practices in the Czech National Awakening." Working Paper. National Council for Eurasian and East European Research. 2012.

Cordini, Lorenzo. "Czech Legends." *My Czech Republic.* n.d.

Demetz, Peter. *Prague in Black and Gold: Scenes from the Life of a European City.* Hill and Wang, 1998.

Dobšinský, Pavol. *Traditional Slovak Folktales.* Ed. and trans. David L. Cooper. M.E. Sharpe, 2001.

Frančíková, Dagmar. "All Czechs, but Particularly Women: The Positionality of Women in the Construction of the Modern Czech Nation, 1820s–1850s." Dissertation. University of Michigan. 2011.

Havel, Václav. *Letters to Olga: June 1979–September 1982.* Trans. Paul Wilson. Henry Holt, 1989.

Higgins, Bernie, and David Vaughan. Interview with Eva Kalivodová. "Božena Němcová—the Mother of Czech Prose." *Radio Prague.* Radio Prague, 31 Oct. 2004.

Hrabal, Bohumil. *Total Fears: Selected Letters to Dubenka.* Trans. James Naughton. Twisted Spoon Press, 1998.

---. *Too Loud a Solitude.* Trans. Michael Henry Heim. Harcourt, 1990.

Iggers, Wilma Abeles. *Women of Prague: Ethnic diversity and social change from the eighteenth century to the present.* Berghahn Books, 1995.

Johnston, Rosie. "Social chronicler and society girl Karolina Světlá." *Radio Prague.* Radio Prague, 29 Aug. 2007.

Kafka, Franz. *Letters to Milena.* Ed. Willy Haas. Trans. Tania and James Stern. Schocken, 1953.

Kočí, Jakub D. *"Teorie: Božena Němcová byla Goyova vnučka. Co vy na to?" Žena-in.* 7 Nov. 2013.

Kundera, Milan. "Three Contexts of Art: From Nation to World." *Cross Currents,* Vol. 12, 1993, pp. 5–14.

Loužil, Jaromír. "Notes on 'the philosophy of love' in *Four Seasons* by Božena Němcová." Trans. Caroline Kovtun. *Slovo a smysl,* or *Word & Sense: A Journal of Interdisciplinary Theory and Criticism in Czech Studies.* Vol. 1, 2004, pp. 356–366.

Nash, Elizabeth. "The Truth About Spanish Art's Most Famous Love Story." *Independent.* 25 Jan. 2007.

Němcová, Božena. *Babička (The Grandmother).* 1855. Trans. Frances Gregor. Vitalis, 2006.

---. "Čtyry doby" ("The Four Seasons"). Trans. by Charles University Introduction to Czech Literature class. *Slovo a smysl,* or *Word & Sense: A Journal of Interdisciplinary Theory and Criticism in Czech Studies.* Vol. 1, 2004, pp. 349–355.

---. "Divá Bára" ("Bewitched Bára"). *Czechoslovak Stories.* Ed. and trans. Šárka B. Hrbková. Duffield, 1920.

---. *The Disobedient Kids and Other Czecho-Slovak Fairy Tales.* Trans. William H. Tolman and V. Smetanka. Koči, 1921.

---. "The Twelve Months." *Muzeum Boženy Němcové.* n.d.

"Němcová, Božena." *Encyclopedia of World Biography.* Gale Group. 2005.

Partridge, James. "Review of *The Grandmother.*" *Central Europe Review.* Vol. 1, No. 7, August 1999.

Peaslee, Margaret H. "Božena Němcová Remembered." *Faculty Page.* U of Pittsburgh, Titusville. n.d.

"Princess Dorothea of Courland." *Wikipedia.* n.d.

"Princess Wilhelmine, Duchess of Sagan." *Wikipedia.* n.d.

Riedlbauchová, Tereza. "'Čtyry doby' by Božena Němcová and 'Čtvero dob' by Tereza Nováková." Trans. and annotator Dana K. Nyvltová. *Jedním Okem/One Eye Open.* 2005.

Rilke, Rainer Maria. *Letters to a Young Poet.* Trans. Joan M. Burnham. New World Library, 2000.

Scott, Ryan. "Dos and Don'ts: Names." *Expats.cz.* 30 May 2011.

Šmejkalová, Jiřina. "Božena Němcová." *Biographical Dictionary of Women's Movements and Feminisms in Central, Eastern, and South Eastern Europe.* Eds. Francisca de Haan, Krassimira Daskalová, and Anna Loutfi. Central European UP, 2006.

Sobková, Helena. *Tajemství Barunky Panklové. Portrét Boženy Němcové.* Mladá Fronta, 1997.

Součková, Milada. *The Czech Romantics.* Mouton, 1958.

"Steidler's Inn." *Muzeum Boženy Němcové.* n.d.

Thomas, Alfred. *Prague Palimpsest: Writing, Memory, and the City.* U of Chicago P, 2010.

Záhoř, Zdeněk. Ed. *Výbor z korespondence Boženy Němcové.* Stanislav Minařík, 1922.

Zipes, Jack. *The Irresistible Fairy Tale: The Cultural and Social History of a Genre.* Princeton UP, 2012.

Acknowledgments

My first and deepest thanks are to Abigail Beckel and Kathleen Rooney of Rose Metal Press, who gave me the freedom and support to create this unique, unusual, and unwieldy book. Under their editorial vision, this multifaceted project gained both structure and depth, and I consider them full collaborators in the process. At each stage they provided insightful nos and yes after generous yes. They have published and promoted two of my books, and I consider them among the most important figures in my writing life.

I am grateful, too, to Heather Butterfield, who also designed *Liliane's Balcony* (with ornaments by Frank Lloyd Wright for each character!), for her stunning design work, attention to detail, and investment in finding the perfect font.

This book incorporates texts from a number of sources, but it draws most extensively on Wilma Iggers' translations of Božena Němcová's correspondence in her excellent book, *Women of Prague: Ethnic Diversity and Social Change from the Eighteenth Century to the Present*. Ms. Iggers graciously gave permission to include her translations in this project. I am grateful to her and to her former editor at Berghahn Books, Ann Przyzycki DeVita.

Grants from the Indiana Arts Commission, the Sustainable Arts Foundation, and Indiana University's Office for the Vice President of International Affairs provided financial support along the way. Excerpts from the book appeared in *Shadowbox* and *Sou'wester*, and the introduction is adapted from "In Search of Božena Němcová," an essay originally published in *The Common*. Many thanks to all of those supporters and editors.

Thanks to the Sedlec Ossuary in Kutná Hora for granting permission to use my photos of the amazing bone sculptures.

Thanks to Joel Langston and his media team at Indiana University South Bend for their work on the book trailer.

Ongoing gratitude goes to my friends and mentors from the University of Cincinnati: Michael Griffith, Nicola Mason, Brock Clarke, Sarah Domet, Kristin Czarnecki, Molly McCaffrey, David Bell, Jody Bates, Darrin Doyle, and Lauren Mosko Bailey. Ten years out and many miles apart, they remain my literary and personal support network. Thanks most especially to Julie Gerk Hernandez, who provided wisdom, tissues, margaritas, and a spare bed during the rough times referred to in this book. These days

I'm thankful for my writing and bowling friends in South Bend: Dionne Irving Bremyer, Aaron Bremyer, David Dodd Lee, and Captain Peaches.

I am grateful for the love and laughter of my family in Ohio and Colorado: Mom, Dad and Pat, Darcy, Dane and Melissa and the boys, and Christian and Travis.

I cherish the memory of my grandparents, Margaret (Hanna) and John Bobrovcan, and I include this photo of my beautiful Granny, who would not fail to notice that there is a photo of Grumpus in this book but not of her.

This book is dedicated to my daughter, Monte, who loves fairy tales and happy endings, but would probably prefer not to have her mother as the protagonist.

And I'm grateful for you, Jake Mattox. You.

About the Author

Kelcey Parker Ervick has traveled to Prague regularly since 2003 and currently directs an overseas study program to Prague and Berlin, where students create collage journals inspired by artists such as Hannah Höch, Toyen (Marie Čermínová), and Jiří Kolář. She is the author of the story collection *For Sale By Owner* (Kore Press) and of *Liliane's Balcony* (Rose Metal Press), a novella-in-flash set at Frank Lloyd Wright's Fallingwater and winner of silver medal awards from the IPPY, Foreword, and Eric Hoffer Book Awards. A recipient of grants from the Indiana Arts Commission and the Sustainable Arts Foundation, she teaches creative writing and literary collage at Indiana University South Bend. Her blog features interviews with contemporary writers and the series, "Letters to Dead Authors": http://phdincreativewriting.wordpress.com.

A Note about the Type

The body text of this book is set in Bajka, a Serbian word that means "fairy tale." Bajka also means "fairy tale" or "fable" in Polish, Czech, and Slovak. Originally designed in 2010 and then released by Serbian type foundry Posterizer KG in 2015, it was created by Lazar Dimitrijević for use in children's fairy tale books. It's a modern interpretation of Baskerville, a transitional typeface, with whimsical, feminine touches. Its literary and Eastern European roots, combined with its fresh form, make it well suited to Parker Ervick's modern and inventive work about a nineteenth-century Czech fairy tale writer.

The footnotes are set in Sofia Pro Condensed, a warmly curved sans serif font that was designed by French graphic designer Olivier Gourvat in 2012, and subsequently released by his Mostardesign Studio. Its strong legibility at a variety of sizes, coupled with its space-saving condensed width, make it a great choice for text that needs to be both small and easily read, like Parker Ervick's editorial footnotes in Part One.

The title on the cover is set in IM Fell DW Pica Pro, a free font designed by Igino Marini and released in 2008. It's a historical revival that's part of Marini's Fell Types collection, which is named after the seventeenth-century Bishop of Oxford and typographer John Fell. The rough, irregular letterforms give the font a charming and rugged character that complements the distressed and layered collage artwork.

—Heather Butterfield